Safe

FROM THE PRIZE-WINNING AUTHOR of *Under the Hawthorn Tree*, a book about twelve-year-old Sophie and her seven-year-old brother, Hugh, who are evacuated from the London Blitz. Dad is away at war, Mum is injured and in hospital, and their home is bombed out. London has become a dangerous place, its streets torn apart, its buildings blown up. Each night there is fear of another attack from the skies. The children are sent to Ireland to stay with a grandfather they have never met, leaving behind them all they have ever known.

**A moving story of children facing
the horrors of war and the heartbreak
of a family feud.**

Special Merit Award to The O'Brien Press
from Reading Association of Ireland
*'for exceptional care, skill and professionalism in
publishing, resulting in a consistently high standard in all
of the children's books published by The O'Brien Press'*

Marita Conlon-McKenna

MARITA CONLON-MCKENNA won an International Reading Association Award (USA) for her novel on the great Irish Famine, *Under the Hawthorn Tree*. She also won the Ostrerreicher Kinder Und Jugendbuchpreis (Austria) and was nominated for Le Prix Litteraire Du Roman Pour Enfants (France). Her work has been translated into many languages, including Japanese, French, Dutch, German, Swedish, Italian, Danish. She lives in Dublin with her husband and four children.

BOOKS PUBLISHED

Under the Hawthorn Tree

Wildflower Girl

Fields of Home

The Blue Horse

No Goodbye

Little Star

Safe Harbour

Marita Conlon-McKenna

THE O'BRIEN PRESS
DUBLIN

First published 1995 by The O'Brien Press Ltd.,
20 Victoria Road, Rathgar, Dublin 6, Ireland.
Tel. +353 1 4923333; Fax. +353 1 4922777
e-mail: books@obrien.ie
website: http://www.obrien.ie
Reprinted 1996, 1997, 1999.

British Library Cataloguing-in-publication Data
Conlon-McKenna, Marita
Safe Harbour
I. Title
823.914 [J]

ISBN 0-86278-422-0

4 6 8 10 9 7 5 3
99 00 02 04 03 01 99 97

Words of 'Goodnight Children Everywhere', by Gabby Rogers and Harry Philips,
reproduced by kind permission of Cecil Lennox Ltd., a Kassner Group company.

The O'Brien Press receives
assistance from

The Arts Council
An Chomhairle Ealaíon

*The characters in this book are fictitious and any resemblance
to any person living or dead is entirely accidental.*

Typesetting, layout, editing, design: The O'Brien Press Ltd.
Printing: Cox & Wyman Ltd., Reading

Contents

Goodnight Children, Everywhere

Goodnight children, everywhere
Your Mummy thinks of you tonight ...
Though you are far away
She's with you night and day.
Goodnight children, everywhere.

Goodnight children, everywhere
Your Daddy thinks of you tonight.
And though you're far away
You'll go home one day.
Goodnight children, everywhere.

Song often broadcast on children's programmes
during World War II

For my mother, Mary

CHAPTER 1

Shelter

Sophie sang.

Her stomach was rumbling and tumbling with the sounds all around her, the high piercing whistle, and the falling of another bomb, then another. She counted, trying to gauge the distance. She wiped the palms of her hands on her blue cotton dress. She felt sweaty and scared. She could feel a damp line of perspiration on her top lip – just as well it wasn't too bright in the air-raid shelter.

They were all singing around her to keep their spirits up. Someone down the row from her had started it. Sophie inhaled a large draft of clammy air and tried to concentrate on the song, letting it swell and ripple through her.

A loud thud resonated through the walls of the shelter and the wooden bench Sophie was sitting on moved and shuddered beneath her. The old woman beside her stirred in her sleep and stopped snoring. She had her slippers on and under her cardigan the pink flannel of her nightie peeked through. Obviously she had been prepared for the night.

'Shove up! Make a bit of room!' A cross-looking woman was trying to get a space for herself. She had a big bag of knitting with her, and she wedged herself in between Sophie and the woman in the nightie. Sophie wondered how she could possibly see enough to knit in the dim light of the oil lamp, but she just clicked and clacked away, not even bothering to look at the stitches at all.

'Hugh!' Sophie said aloud, suddenly remembering her seven-year-old brother. Her eyes scanned the crowd around her. Finally she spotted him down at the far end of the shelter with an assorted group of kids. Someone had whitewashed the walls of the shelter, and the 'painting lady' was there again, with her tins of paint and big chunky bristle brushes, amusing the smaller children. Hugh was semi-crouched, down low, trying to paint what looked like a giant orange butterfly.

'Think of the colours! Think of the light! Think of the air blowing in the garden!' said the painting lady cheerfully.

'Yes, Miss Joyce!' the little children all chorused.

Sophie smiled to herself. Even in the half-light and from a distance, she could see that some of the butterflies were already being transformed into Hurricane and Messerschmidt fighter planes, looping through the sky. It didn't matter what the little ones painted – flowers, birds, butterflies – somehow or other they could not escape what was happening above their heads, across the skies of England.

Sophie closed her eyes, trying not to think about it all. Then she heard a loud explosion, followed shortly by another. The whole shelter juddered and everyone went quiet.

'Go on! Give 'em hell!' a man shouted finally, as anti-aircraft guns rat-tat-tatted out in reply to the German Luftwaffe.

Night after night the same thing happened. It seemed as if it was never going to stop. The Germans were determined to destroy the whole city of London, building by building, bit by bit, night after night.

The knitting woman began a chant:

> *'London Bridge is falling down,*
> *Falling down, falling down ...'*

Sophie joined in, singing it low, to herself, then the old lady beside her moved and began to sing it too, in her half-sleep:

> *'London town is falling down,*
> *falling down, falling down,*
> *London town is falling down,*
> *My fair lady.*
>
> *We'll build it up with bricks and stone ...'*

Gradually more voices joined in. As soon as they finished one song, someone would start another.

> *'Humpty Dumpty sat on a wall ...'*

All the old nursery rhymes – 'Old MacDonald Had a Farm', 'Lavender Blue'. Songs of comfort.

The shelter filled with voices. If you sang, you blocked out the noises, the 'bad' noises.

'You've a fine voice, dear! Sweet, but strong.' The old lady, fully awake now, took a triangle of paper from her pocket and held it towards Sophie. 'Mint humbugs! Good for the throat! Go on, have one!'

Sophie stretched her two fingers in. The sweets were so sticky she had to prise them apart. Eventually she got one

11

and popped it in her mouth.

The old lady nodded, satisfied. Sophie sucked her humbug. Her tongue told her that a bit of paper from the wrapping was still stuck to it, but she didn't care.

Hugh ran over to her, pushing his hair back off his forehead. He had smears of paint on his hands and a yellow streak across his brow.

He stared at Sophie's mouth. 'What you got?'

'A sweet,' she replied.

The old lady ignored him. The sweets were back in her pocket and she wasn't going to offer any more.

'I'm hungry,' he whined.

Sophie didn't like to remind him that it was because of his dawdling at his friend Simon's house that they had missed tea and were now stuck in this public shelter, just two streets away from home.

'I want to go home!' Hugh insisted.

Sophie said nothing.

'Now! Right now, Soph! I want –' He stopped suddenly as everyone gasped with one breath. An enormous bang resounded through the shelter. It must be a hit, definitely. They all felt it, really close by. Could it be *their* street? Sophie wondered in a panic.

'When it's over, Hugh,' she said in a shaky voice, 'when the All Clear sounds – but it's not over yet.'

He squatted down on his haunches near her, quiet now. If only he would fall asleep the time would go far quicker, Sophie thought. All the kids were getting scrappy and bored.

The painting was finished and now left to dry, abandoned. Miss Joyce was busy repacking the stuff in a box. Then, like a magician, she produced a bagful of buns and walked around offering one to each child.

Hugh helped himself to a cherry bun.

Miss Joyce stopped in front of Sophie. 'Go on, take one!'

Sophie nodded her thanks.

Miss Joyce was part of the Women's Voluntary Service, judging by her uniform. 'Looks like we'll be here for the night,' she said. 'There's no sign of this letting up at all.'

Sophie tried to hide her dismay, but Miss Joyce noticed. 'Are your parents with you?'

'No,' Sophie replied. 'I was on my way home from collecting my brother Hugh when the sirens started so we just made a dash for here. It's much earlier than usual, and there wasn't enough time to get home.'

'Much better to be safe here, though I'm sure your parents will be worried. Do you know where they are?'

'Dad's away in the war ... and, you see, there's an Anderson shelter in our back garden,' Sophie explained, 'that's where we usually go. Mum'll be there.'

'Well, dear, you're here now so you'd better make the most of it,' recommended Miss Joyce, before moving off to talk to a young mother and her new baby.

Sophie yawned and stretched. Back in their own shelter she had a blanket and pillow, and a proper lamp and a pile of her favourite books and some paper and a pen and pencils to do her homework. Here, she was stuck with nothing – and she was responsible for Hugh!

Around her, heads were beginning to nod again. The singing had died away. The knitting needles clicked and clacked again. The air was getting stuffier and smellier. Sophie managed to turn sideways and squeeze Hugh in beside her. Pulling off her green knitted cardigan, she made a pillow to rest her head against. Hugh kept moaning on and on about the place, but eventually he gave up and slept.

All night the sounds continued, the whinny of one bomb falling after another. Each time Sophie's heart raced and pounded against her ribs, and she tried not to think of the ground above them falling in and burying them all alive. She could hear the sirens and fire engines and muffled shouts as well as the rumbling drones of attacking aircraft well into the night.

CHAPTER 2

All Clear

'Sophie! Wake up!' Hugh was standing over her, shaking her.

The All Clear sounded.

'It's time to go home,' he announced.

She was stiff and sore. The shoulder of her dress was damp from leaning against the wall. Sophie made an attempt to smoothen her hair, and she shook out her crumpled cardigan and dragged it on. Hugh had bags under his eyes from tiredness, and his mouse-fair hair stood on end. She spat on her fingers to try and flatten it down. The paint stain on his forehead had faded a bit, but he did look a sight.

In future she was always going to carry a comb with her, she decided. Honestly, they looked like two tramps.

Some people were changing their clothes now. Others lay wrapped in blankets still fast asleep, unaware of, or ignoring the early-morning movements around them.

Deftly, Sophie and Hugh made their way to the entrance, picking their steps over the sleepers, and following the crowd upwards and onto the street.

The hazy morning light made them both blink, and the fresh air made them yawn. They gulped in the cold morning air as they got used to being back outside.

'Crikey!' Hugh stood rigid, pointing, his eyes almost popping out of his head.

The whole corner of shops across from the shelter was gone, collapsed into a massive sagging heap of bricks and timber and dust. Smoke sputtered from gas fires that flared from the broken gas mains, which looked like a giant octopus pushing its way up from underneath the pavement. Two or three firemen moved among the debris.

Sophie tried not to think of Mr Brady, the butcher. He had a shop there and lived overhead with his family. She hadn't seen him in the shelter.

'Mr Bones – his shop's gone! Do you think he's all right, Sophie?' stammered Hugh.

She nodded, trying to block out the smiling face and kindness of the man in the white apron, who always managed to sneak their mother a bit more meat than the ration book allowed. A few sausages, a nice bit of beef, a small chicken – just because they were part-Irish like himself.

Sophie didn't want to see the wreckage of his home and business. 'Come on, Hugh! Mum will be worried sick.'

But Hugh was standing, mouth open with curiosity, pointing to a one-storey section of an office which was almost swaying. 'Can't we wait a minute? Maybe the rest of it will fall,' he pleaded.

'No! We can't! Now stop dawdling and come on home!' She grabbed his sleeve and pulled him after her.

The street behind where they lived was cordoned off. It was a No Go area. Sophie was almost too scared to look as they reached the end of their own street. The street-warden stood there, chatting to a small group of men, and the children managed to slip by them.

'Mind where you go, you two!' Mr Thompson, their neighbour, roared after them. 'You kids shouldn't be out until we survey the damage here.'

Sophie couldn't help running as they got nearer to their own house. There was no sign of life. The black-out curtains were still down, and everything seemed very quiet, almost as if the whole of Grove Avenue were still asleep. A shower of dust clung to the front windows, to the redbrick walls and to the blue hall door of number seven, their house.

Sophie had a spare key and let herself into the dark hallway, shouting up the stairs: 'Mum! We're home! We had to stay in the shelter on Bury Road!'

There was no reply, and Sophie became aware of that still, strange feeling of an empty house.

Hugh ran down the passageway and pushed open the kitchen door. Plaster and dust rained down on his head, and he put his arms up to protect himself. The kitchen table was set for three, and a plate of buttered bread sat there, curled and hard, mocking them, as bits of upstairs lay scattered around the floor. The scullery door and window no longer existed, and Sophie warned Hugh to be careful of the shards of glass, as every window at the back of the house seemed to have been blown in.

'Where's Mum?' Hugh cried.

'She's probably out in the shelter with Mrs Abercorn,' Sophie tried to convince herself.

They tiptoed carefully through the opening where the back

door had been, making their way to the back garden through the yard. The fence between the two small semi-detached houses had been let collapse over the years, and the man from the Ministry had organised putting a shelter between the two houses, so they could share it.

Their next-door neighbour, Flossie Abercorn, was a widow and a really nice old lady. She had watched the men erecting the shelter and kept saying, 'Well, I never!'

The man from the Ministry had shown them leaflets with pictures and drawings of how to make good use of the shelter, and how some people grew cabbages and carrots and scallions and all sorts of produce over the roof and sides of theirs.

Flossie Abercorn shook her head. 'It's bad enough having to run like rabbits underground because of "Gerry", but I have no intention of being found dead and buried under a pile of cabbages and cauliflowers and the like. It's not respectable at my age.' No one knew her exact age, but it was old.

Mrs Abercorn had planted flower bulbs and seeds and cuttings instead. 'We'll have a fine show here in the summer, just you wait and see,' she told Mum and Dad – her own version of 'Dig for Victory'.

Sophie made her way to the forget-me-not- and wallflower-covered mound. Hugh chased on ahead. For an instant Sophie looked back. Even their roof sagged.

'Hugh! Be careful,' she warned again.

'Mum! Mrs Abercorn! It's us, Hugh and Sophie.' Hugh scrambled down into the Anderson shelter.

'Oh! Hugh, pet!' cried their neighbour, hugging the boy, 'I thought my end had come! One of them bombs must have landed almost on top of me. Tell me, is the house still standing? Where's your mother? Where were you all? I was ever so worried. I ...'

'It's all right, Mrs Abercorn, we ... we're both fine,' said Sophie.

The old lady looked frightened and haggard. Her hands were shaking and she seemed very unwell. She dabbed at her eyes with a crumpled old hankie. 'I was so scared all on my own!'

'Sit down, Mrs Abercorn. You're all right and we're here with you now,' soothed Sophie. She really wanted to shake the old woman and find out where her Mum was, but knew it wouldn't help matters. She motioned to Hugh.

'Go get Mr Thompson!'

Her brother disappeared back outside to run for help.

'You'll be fine, Mrs Abercorn ... a nice cup of tea ... plenty of sugar ... a warm bed ...'

The woman was so cold now that her teeth were chattering. 'I'll be fine, love ... d ... d ... don't you worry!'

Sophie stood watching to see if there was any sign of the warden coming. Her eyes searched the yard and patchy garden. Water sputtered from the broken pipe of the outside tap. A bicycle tyre lay on its own and it took a few seconds before she realised that it was from Hugh's bike. The rope of the washing line was scattered across the grass where an enormous crater had appeared. Bits of their green hedge blew like tumbleweed ... then Sophie became aware of the strange bundle of clothes scattered haphazardly along the path and the stretched doll-like figure in the middle of it all.

'Mummy!'

She began to run.

CHAPTER 3

The Home Front

Mum lay totally still, as if she were fast asleep. Sophie was too scared to disturb her as she watched the tremulous rise and fall of her mother's breathing and the tiny throb of pulse in her neck. One of her legs lay at an awkward angle.

'Mum! It's me! It's Sophie!'

She could not tell if her mother could hear her or not. Funny, but she looked perfect except for the dark stain of blood on the path under her, which clung to her hair and ear. The grey school-jumper she had knit for Hugh lay loosely beside her.

'You'll be fine, Mum! Hugh's gone to get help. Please, Mum. I love you.'

Sophie stroked the shabby pink cardigan her mother wore and pulled the faded floral print skirt down, covering her thighs. She felt dizzy and sick herself, and the pain in her chest was so strong that she could hardly breathe or swallow. Someone came up behind her.

'It's all right, lass! You did the right thing not to move her. Never move a head injury. The ambulance will be here in a jiffy.' Mr Thompson knelt down and took hold of her mother's wrist to check her pulse.

'Will she be all right, Mr Thompson?'

The warden pretended not to hear her.

Slow, silent tears slid down Sophie's face and plopped on to the dust-covered path. She sniffed and wished she had a hankie. The warden passed her one.

'Go on, lass! Have a good blow!'

She shoved it up her sleeve afterwards.

'Any minute now, my love. They'll be here any minute now, Mrs Fitzpatrick, you just hang on, my love, and they'll have you in the hospital in no time.' He rambled on, talking soothingly to her mother.

Sophie turned to discover Hugh, panting and out of breath from all the running, standing dazed behind her.

'She's alive, Hugh! She's still alive!' she shouted at him, but he didn't seem to take it in.

A woman from the Women's Voluntary Service and a member of the Home Guard appeared. The woman put her arm around Hugh and led him to where Mrs Abercorn was sitting, wrapped in a big thick red blanket.

'Best to get that old dear to the hospital!' the warden said to the man from the Home Guard. 'Ticker trouble by the look of it.'

Two more women in uniform appeared. They seemed very sure of what to do, and Sophie stood out of their way as they produced a stretcher and gently rolled her mother on to it. Mum looked terribly white and her eyes were still shut. Mr Thompson helped them to lift the stretcher through the back garden, and out to the front where an ambulance lay waiting. Two or three neighbours were standing around.

'I must go with her!' insisted Sophie.

'I'm sorry, dear,' replied the peroxide-blond lady who was driving, 'I'm afraid we're full up. We were already on our way to Saint Martin's Hospital when we were diverted here, so we've a full load. I'm sorry!'

'But ...!' Sophie didn't know what to say.

'I'm sorry,' the lady said firmly, climbing up into the driving seat and refusing to discuss it any further.

'Best to stay and mind your brother, lass,' urged the warden. 'We'll get you to the hospital later, I promise. Word of honour!'

Sophie had to believe Mr Thompson, as she watched the white lorry with its red cross swerve and lurch off down the road.

CHAPTER 4

Bombed Out

The recreation centre was packed. It was really the old parish hall, where jumble sales and meetings and choir practice and the drama society took place. But now it had been transformed into a place of rest for those who had nowhere else to go. The huge room had been divided up, and a makeshift canteen set up at one end, where volunteers were busy doling out hot breakfasts and mugs of tea to those in need. A few tables and chairs had been grouped together and Sophie recognised one or two of the families sitting there.

In one corner a gang of toddlers played together, and the far end of the room contained two rows of camp beds, neatly laid out. Some had been slept in, and others lay ready for use.

Mr Thompson had brought Sophie and Hugh to the centre. 'Bombed out!' he announced to Mrs Stokes, the woman in charge. 'Right old shock they've had. The mother's been taken off to the hospital.'

'Mrs Stokes will take good care of you both now,' he said to them. 'I'll be back up to see you later. I've got to get back to Grove Avenue, and get the engineers to have a look at that house of yours – and the rest of the street.'

Sophie's heart sank. So he *did* think their house was unsafe. It would be cordoned off until they decided if it had to be demolished or not. The house where they had lived all their lives ...

'Come on, ducks! Let's get you both a cup of tea and a bite of breakfast!' interrupted Mrs Stokes. She was sturdily built, and seemed to be a really calm type of person, who didn't get in a flap about things.

In a few minutes she had them sitting down, with two big mugs of milky tea and a plate of fried bread and some baked beans in front of them.

'Would you care for anything else to eat?' she enquired.

Hugh simply shook his head.

'No, thank you,' replied Sophie, kicking her brother on the shins to remind him of his good manners.

'You both look all done in,' said Mrs Stokes, 'so I'll arrange for you to lie down when you've finished.'

'No!' exclaimed Sophie, almost shouting at her. 'I don't want to lie down. I must stay awake! There might be news of my Mum.'

'Look, Sophie! I promise you the very minute there is any news I'll wake you, and I promise to take you to the hospital too.'

Sophie nodded dumbly. She felt such a big sissy because she wanted to cry again. She just longed to be back in their small messy house in Grove Avenue.

'Another drop of tea?' asked Mrs Stokes kindly. 'Your brother is nearly asleep already, so go on, you go and lie down too, now that you've eaten.'

Sophie dragged the two campbeds close beside each other.

Hugh was strangely quiet, almost as if he was afraid to ask any questions for fear of the answers he'd get.

People lay on the beds chatting. 'The whole street gutted ... that's what I heard ... not a brick left standing!'

'Water flooding everywhere!'

'Decent people ... why do they do such things?'

'Shot down over the channel.'

Snatches of conversation drifted around her, and under the blanket, Sophie held Hugh's hand.

'It's all right, Hugh! We're together, that's all that matters.'

Sophie stirred. Mrs Stokes was bending towards her.

'What time is it?' she asked sleepily.

'Three o'clock.'

'Oh no! I've been asleep for hours,' she sighed.

'I came down to tell you we've just had word about your mother,' Mrs Stokes told them gently. 'She had surgery and is in the intensive care section, but she has pulled through.'

Sophie blessed herself. 'When can I see her?'

'Me too?' demanded Hugh.

'Well, I can't say for certain, but Mr Thompson will be waiting for you at Saint Martin's. I'll be knocking off duty in about half an hour, and I can drop you there, on my way home.'

'Oh! Thank you, Mrs Stokes. I appreciate it!' said Sophie, with a lump in her throat.

'I 'preciate it too,' murmured Hugh, copying her.

CHAPTER 5

Damage

Mrs Stokes's car was packed to the roof with stuff.

There were cardboard boxes everywhere, containing bandages, antiseptic, tea, spare sheets.

'Squash in!' she told them brightly. 'Push that mess out of your way!'

But there was nowhere to push all the supplies, and they ended up practically sitting on the things, trying not to squash them.

'I love this old jalopy,' Mrs Stokes confided as the engine of the Morris spluttered into life.

On the way to the hospital she rabbited on about her family – her husband who worked fairly high-up in the War Office, her daughter Gwen who was a nurse, Helen who was studying in Oxford, and her son Tim who was a trainee pilot, and had been on four missions already.

'Wish I was a pilot!' sighed Hugh.

'Not in these times, pet! Not in these times, Hugh, when the skies are so dangerous and have become a battlefield,' warned Mrs Stokes, her voice choked with emotion.

As if to distract herself, she pointed out the damage done by the previous night's raid, as they drove past.

'Senseless waste!' she muttered.

Finally they came to a halt outside Saint Martin's, a looming grey stone Victorian building, which gave Sophie the creeps. She had been here once before, about four years ago when she was eight, and had got a big splinter of wood from a swing stuck in her backside. She blushed even thinking of it and hoped that none of the doctors or nurses would remember her. She tried to let her straight brown hair partially cover her face as Mrs Stokes led them into the waiting area.

'Mr Thompson will be along in a while, Sophie, and maybe one of the nurses. Sorry I've got to rush off, but I've got a million things to do. Anyway, I'll see you both at breakfast time tomorrow in the centre, when I'm back on duty.' Sophie wished she could stay with them. 'Don't worry, Sophie! Ah look, there's the warden!' Mrs Stokes reassured her, going over to him to have a word.

Sophie and Hugh sat quietly on the bench waiting. They counted the windows, the black-out panels, the patterned black and white and green tiles in the corridor.

'I hate hospitals,' murmured Hugh.

Every now and then a cry or a moan of pain would issue from some open door. Nurses in uniform and doctors in white coats with stethoscopes hanging around their necks passed by. People in wheelchairs or on crutches slowly made their way along; visitors strode by in a hurry, knowing where they were going; and shambling old folk hung about, obviously waiting for news of relations.

Sophie tried not to focus on it, but she hated the smell of disinfectant and heaven knows what else, and of potato and cabbage and corned beef that filled the air around them.

'Ah, there you are!' Mr Thompson finally came towards them, a nurse in uniform following behind.

'Sophie! Hugh! This is Nurse Harvey. She's helping to look after your mother.'

The nurse smiled at them. 'Come along,' she said, and led them all up a wide stone staircase for two floors until they reached a long white corridor. Nurse Harvey stopped.

'Now, you must both promise me to be very quiet,' she said. 'Your mother is in a ward with five other patients and I'm afraid they're all seriously ill. She's in a very deep sleep, and we're not sure if she's able to hear. I'll let you see her for a few minutes, and then we'll have a chat in my office.'

Sophie hardly dared to breathe when she walked into the big room. Everything was white – the walls, the floor, the uniforms, the sheets, the bandages around her mother's head, the white cage thing over her plastered-up leg. And her mother lay looking bluish-white in the middle of it all.

A voice which seemed to be plucked out of the air said: 'Mum, it's me. Sophie. Hugh's here too. We're both fine. We want you to get well. You're in hospital, you know the one you brought me to the time of the swing, you and Dad ...' she trailed off.

'Mum! Mummee!' Hugh's voice was urgent, pleading. 'Mum, wake up!' Forgetting the warnings, he was trying to half-hug, half-shake her by the shoulder. 'I love you, Mummy! Wake up! Please!'

Nurse Harvey rushed over and managed to quieten him, then she led him back to Mr Thompson, who took him by the hand. Sophie could hear his half-crying echo down the corridor and stairs. 'I want her to wake up ... wake up!'

Sophie bit her lip and touched her mother's long fingers that lay stretched out on top of the cover. She was aware of the nurse standing at the door watching her closely.

'I love you, Mum. You have to rest now and get better. Don't worry about us. We have somewhere to stay.'

Nurse Harvey came over and whispered to her to come away now, and she led her back outside into a small pokey office with a desk and two chairs. On the wall was a large drawing of a human body and a chart of emergency procedures. Nurse Harvey coughed.

'Well, Sophie, I'm glad to see you're a sensible girl with a cool head on you. I think it's best for me to tell you about your mother's condition. I believe you were the one who found her?'

Sophie nodded.

'Well, first of all, you probably noticed her leg and the cage over it. She has fractured the right femur,' the nurse pointed to the drawing on the wall, 'and also broken two of her toes. The force of the bomb probably flung her to the ground, so she did this as she fell. Perhaps something struck off her foot, we don't know. These will set, and be fine in a few weeks' time. The more serious injury is to her head. Obviously she hit it off something hard.'

'The concrete path to our washing line,' Sophie offered.

'Possibly. With the impact, she fractured her skull. The brain, as you know, lies inside the skull, the shell that protects it –'

'Like an egg,' said Sophie.

'Yes, and with a bad blow the brain can swell, fluid can leak, pressure can build up. We can relieve some of the pressure, and hope to stop internal bleeding, but after that it's time and nature and a lot of good nursing. It's too early to tell yet ...'

'Will she live?' asked Sophie anxiously.

'Oh, Sophie, we do hope so! We think so, but she *is* very ill. At present she's in a state of coma. We can't say how long that will continue.'

'Is my mother in pain?'

'As far as we can know, we don't think so. And she's having pain relief. The next few days will tell us a lot.'

'How long will she be here?'

'I can't really say yet, but it may be a long time. The brain is a very delicate organ, it takes time to heal.'

Sophie stared at the pile of charts on the desk. Libby Fitzpatrick, her mother's name, was written on the top.

'There's a lot for you to take in today,' Nurse Harvey added kindly. 'I'll talk to you when you're in again. You know, new research is showing that hearing a familiar voice and familiar sounds are good sometimes for people in your mother's condition. So you must come again – but I think, for the moment, it's best not to bring your younger brother.'

Sophie nodded.

'Oh, before you go, I have a parcel here with some of your mother's things. You might like to take them with you.' She passed a small brown paper parcel across the desk to Sophie.

Sophie thanked her, and left the office.

She stopped on the first landing, and leant against the heavy leaded stained-glass window depicting some saint, probably Saint Martin, and peered into the bag. Not much: the check apron her mother wore when cleaning or cooking; a handwritten recipe for rabbit and potato pie; a ration-card holder – Sophie had embroidered it for her as a gift, with the initials L.F. surrounded by bluebells; her mother's watch, its face cracked; and a gap-toothed comb, a few coins, the gold cross and chain her mother always wore, and, underneath everything, Hugh's school-jumper. Mum had gone to endless trouble to get fine-quality grey wool for it, as the heavier wool made him itch. It had a v-neck with a pale blue line around it. It had been knitted last year, and already was almost outgrown and beginning to look small. It still felt damp, and had a clothes peg attached to it. Sophie shoved it back into the paper bag. She guessed that her mother had been trying to get that stupid jumper off the washing line when ...

Sophie scrunched her eyes shut. Then she glanced up at the window. The glass saint stared down at her.

'You! You'd better take care of my mother! Do you hear me?' she shouted as she ran off down the stairs.

CHAPTER 6

St Martin's

Sophie ate her breakfast, scrambled powdered eggs – ugh! – and a mugful of steaming tea that had been stewing in a big urn since early morning.

The centre was crowded. She and Hugh had spent the night in the shelter again, and she was bleary-eyed from the lack of solid sleep. Hugh was still out for the count on the camp bed.

About twenty children from the district were about to be evacuated to the country, far away from the dangers of London, and they were hopping around the place with excitement. Mrs Stokes, she knew, was hoping to get herself and Hugh evacuated too, but Sophie decided to avoid discussing it with her until her mother's condition improved. She was staying put in London.

'I'm off to the hospital,' Sophie mouthed to Reverend Fry later that morning. He was reading Bible stories to some of the younger kids. Hugh was engrossed in the story of Noah's Ark, and luckily didn't whine to come with her.

The weather was crisp and cool outside. She would walk today and save money. There was a queue outside Baxters, the high-street grocers. The women were standing patiently with their shopping bags, gossiping. Sugar and some bacon and maybe cheese, that's what they were hoping would be on offer today. That's what the rumours had said anyway. Normally Sophie would have joined the line, but now she didn't need to. She was forced to slow down as part of the street had given way to a curious pattern of holes and cracks. The path would occasionally give a strange wobble under the weight of her feet, threatening to send her sprawling in the dust.

Work crews were busy trying to salvage gas pipes which lay twisted and torn amid the concrete. The railings all along Windsor Terrace were gone, obviously off to a munitions factory to be melted down. Things were getting worse all over Europe, with sea battles, air battles, land battles. What would they do if the Germans invaded Britain? wondered Sophie.

The doctor and matron were busy in her mother's ward. Sophie would have to wait, and she decided to pop down to see Mrs Abercorn. This ward was much bigger than her mother's, with about sixteen old ladies arranged around the room in beds, and a few sitting in wheelchairs.

Mrs Abercorn hugged her tight.

'Oh Sophie, pet! I'm ever so pleased to see you. How is your poor mother?'

'She's a little better. She opened her eyes last time. I think she knew me because she said my name,' Sophie confided.

'Oh, thank God!' the old lady smiled.

Sophie suddenly realised that Mrs Abercorn was indeed a very old lady. She seemed to have shrunk, and her hands and arms and neck were far bonier than Sophie remembered.

'I'll be getting my marching orders in a few days,' Mrs Abercorn announced.

'Are you going home?' Sophie asked.

'No, no, pet! The old place is all bombed out, just like yours – unsafe, they tell me. No, I'm going to Eastbourne, to a convalescent home for old folks like myself. My sister Millie and her husband Ron live about twenty miles from there.'

'Oh!' said Sophie.

'We all have to do our bit, part of the war effort. Have to put up with things. You know something, love, I haven't stayed a night out of London since I was sixteen. Young Joe was always trying to coax me to come over to Canada, said he wanted to show off his old Mum, but I couldn't do it, just couldn't leave London. I reckon old Adolf has changed my mind for me. Still, there's life in the old bird yet. They haven't finished me off yet!'

Sophie grinned to herself, Mrs Abercorn was a tough old girl, and she would miss her terribly.

'Aunt Jessie!' Sophie couldn't believe it. Jessie, her mother's younger sister, was sitting in the chair beside Mum's bed. She almost squashed the breath out of Sophie with a tight squeezing hug. 'I'm so glad to see you, Sophie!'

Mum was half-sitting up, propped up with pillows against

the bed-rest. She opened her eyes drowsily and tried to smile.

'Oh Libby! You smiled at me!' Aunt Jessie murmured proudly.

Sophie was so relieved to see her aunt. It didn't matter that she was a scatterbrain and not to be relied on. She was an adult member of the family, and she had turned up.

They sat by her mother's bed for over an hour. Aunt Jessie kept telling stories of when they were children, and the trouble they used to get into, and talked about how beautiful Mum was on her wedding day. Sophie gave her a kick when she mentioned the house. Sometimes Mum would nod, and her sister would squeeze her fingers and pat her arm.

Mum was tired and eventually the blue eyes closed heavily and her breathing became deeper and she slept.

'Let's go get a cup of tea!' mouthed her aunt.

They walked silently from the hospital, and found a small tea shop round the corner. After a few minutes, the waitress, in her black uniform and starched white apron, got them a seat near the window. Aunt Jessie almost flung herself on it and immediately reached into her handbag, got out a packet of cigarettes and lit up, puffing the smoke into the air.

'Ah! That's better!' she joked, running her free hand through her shoulder-length bob of curling brown hair. 'Sophie! Tell me how you've been, and my little man, Hugh? I got such a scare when I heard what happened!'

'We're staying at the centre on Bury Road. The old church hall.'

'I know,' said Aunt Jessie. 'I spoke to a Mrs Stokes on the

phone. Listen, Sophie, something has got to be sorted out for you and Hugh. They want to evacuate you to somewhere safe, and I can't say I blame them. I haven't seen London since I came to stay with you last Christmas. The whole place is in bits, falling apart – shops, buildings, offices, homes, just gone – honestly, I could have cried when I got off the train today. Anyway, it's no place for a pair of kids, whatever about those that have to stay and work in the city.'

'I won't leave Mum!' shouted Sophie, making the two old ladies beside them turn and stare. 'I'm not leaving Mum!' she muttered obstinately.

Her aunt puffed long and slow on the cigarette.

'You saw your Mum today, Sophie! It's doctors and nurses she needs most at the moment, they're the ones who'll get her better. Soon she'll start to worry about the two of you. Libby is a worrier, you know that, and she'll worry and make herself even more ill. She called Hugh's name twice in her sleep. You know what she's like, Sophie!'

Sophie nodded. Her aunt was right. 'Couldn't we go and live with you, please?' she pleaded.

'You know, darling, that I'd love to have you, but I have no house or place of my own. I gave up the flat I shared with Helen and Rose when my office transferred out of the city. I just couldn't afford to keep on paying the rent for Museum Square. You won't believe it, but at the moment we've been released from desk duties and are all working as "landgirls".'

Sophie laughed. Anyone more unlike a 'landgirl' was hard to imagine.

'I know!' her aunt blushed and sipped her tea. 'You should see me in my overalls and wellies, up to my knees in mud and heaven knows what else!'

'We were evacuated before, you know, with Mum,' Sophie reminded her. 'Remember, we went to stay with that ghastly Mrs Monks outside Oxford. She starved us almost and wouldn't let Mum have any hot water to wash in. Even the walls of the bedroom were damp. It was disgusting, and when Dad saw it he took us back home immediately.'

'That was different, Soph! Things had got quiet then and Neil thought it was safe for you again in London. But now things are a whole lot worse. Libby should have sent you away earlier. I don't know what she was thinking of!'

'I don't want to be evacuated! I don't want to leave London!' As soon as she said it, an image of old Mrs Abercorn flashed across Sophie's mind.

'The Luftwaffe are stepping things up, Sophie. Hitler is pushing as hard as he can and the whole of Europe, as we know it, is falling into his hands. He intends to destroy London, and every man, woman or child that stands in his way. That's what everyone says. Please, Sophie, we've all got to think about what's best.'

Sophie knew in her heart of hearts that her aunt was right. Aunt Jessie was never serious, but now Sophie realised that there was no budging her. Thousands of children were being evacuated – why should they be any different?

'I've written to Neil, and I wrote to your grandfather, and also telephoned him.'

'*Grandfather?*' Sophie almost choked on her tea.

'Yes, your grandfather in Ireland. I told him about Libby's condition and he has agreed to take yourself and Hugh.'

Grandfather, how are you! To Sophie all he was was someone who sent a Christmas card with a pound note in it every year. His letters were few and far between. Her father refused to look at them, and her mother would sit brooding and hunched, reading them, and afterwards lock them away in the mahogany bureau. The night after a letter came there was always a row between her parents, and Sophie had come to dread their arrival with the tell-tale Irish stamp and postmark.

'But we've never even seen him! He doesn't know us or care about us! Why should we have to go to bloody Ireland?'

'Sophie! He is your grandfather, after all, your flesh and blood. Libby did keep in touch with him, you know. She told me she wrote to him sometimes,' her aunt said earnestly. 'You could go off and be evacuated to God knows where and to anybody, like you were in Oxford, or you have a chance to go to Ireland to someone who's related to you. It's where your father was reared, and besides, Ireland is a safe place. The prime minister, Mr De Valera, has declared its neutrality.'

Sophie sat, silent.

'Kids!' muttered Aunt Jessie, pouring herself another cup of tea.

'I'll think about it!' Sophie said grudgingly.

CHAPTER 7

Movietone News

Sophie hated the war! It had changed everything, turned her world topsy turvey, upside down, like sand shifting beneath your feet.

She thought about it all as she sat in the local park. It wasn't a big important park like Hyde Park, or Regent's Park, but it too had changed. They had taken all the railings down, and melted them. Imagine using the park railings to make guns and weapons to kill people! She wondered if they did the same thing in the parks in Germany. The whole world had gone crazy.

Normally at this time of year, when the cherry blossom drifted like snow through the air, the park would be crowded. Today it was half-empty – only a few old people, and a couple of mothers and toddlers, and a nurse, in her starched uniform, pushing a big fancy pram up and down in the spring sunshine.

Sophie sat on the wooden bench, watching the small collection of ducks paddling in the pond, every now and then darting their heads beneath its murky surface.

She had so much to think about: Mum sick in the hospital, her head swathed in bandages, and no nurse or doctor able to say for definite how long it was going to take for her to get better. Dad had put on his uniform and marched away like a thousand other dads, to fight in this bloody war. Mum had begged him not to go. 'You're Irish, Neil. It's not your fight.' But all he said was: 'I have lived and worked here in England for almost twenty years, the woman I love is English, my children have been born and reared here – no madman is going to destroy the people and place I love. Libby, I have to fight. This *is* my fight, I have to protect me and mine.' And so her Dad had gone, like all the other dads, like Mr Brown the park-keeper – normally these beds would be a riot of colour by now, but there were only a few straggly tulips and some freesia here and there, and clumps of daring weeds pushed their way up all over the place. And the lawns were in dire need of a cut.

Even St Martin's Academy, Sophie and Hugh's school, had changed. The children came in late and most of them spent half the morning yawning. Some days classes were almost full, and on others only a few pupils would turn up. It all depended on the pattern of the bombing the night before. And then children began to disappear – evacuated, or worse? Sophie couldn't bear to think of it. All her friends going.

Homework was meant to be done, but what teacher was going to scold someone who had spent most of the night in an air-raid shelter? Sophie found that it was hardly worth the bother of making an effort to work. And usually every year the school put on a big show, the summer show, but that too had been cancelled. It was silly and selfish, Sophie knew, to be upset because she hadn't the chance to audition, the chance to sing. There was no guarantee she would have got a part anyway – but she was a good singer and everyone praised her voice. Even the choir had been suspended.

'It's only a temporary suspension,' Miss Oliver, the singing teacher, had assured them, but nobody really believed her.

Sophie hated being late, hated homework not done, subjects being changed, rules broken.

'Sophie! You're a creature of habit!' her Dad had teased, giving her a hug, making her smile.

A creature of habit! Maybe that was just a nice way of saying that she was dull, ordinary and boring – with straight brown hair and a squared-off chin, and lips that were just a bit too big, and pale white skin with a squiggle of freckles across her nose and cheeks, which she hated.

I'm just like that duck, she thought, a plain old ordinary duck. The duck swam back and forth, dabbling among the pondweed, its brown eyes glinting as it searched for food for itself and its young. Its beige-brown plumage blended with its surroundings as it weaved through the water.

So, she and Hugh were to be sent away to Ireland, to a grandfather they didn't know, who probably hated them. To a strange country, to a strange man who would not even speak to his own son. Grown-ups didn't care – maybe they had forgotten what it was like. Sophie was scared. Scared because of this bloody war, because everything was changing.

It was all settled. Aunt Jessie and Mrs Stokes and the other women had talked on and on about it.

Sophie was angry with them. People should mind their own business and not go poking their noses into other people's lives.

Hugh was easily bought off. A big bag of sticky toffees and a few squares of fudge and he had listened, wide-eyed and unprotesting, when their aunt told him about being evacuated again.

'Where are we going?' he asked Sophie, cheeks and jaws bulging.

'Ireland,' she stated flatly.

'Where's that?' he asked as he munched.

'Across the Irish sea, bloody miles away.'

Aunt Jessie was trying to make amends. 'What about a trip to the cinema, you two? Would you like that, Hugh?'

Hugh nodded. Sophie simply fumed away in silence.

The Odeon was packed and Sophie sat on the edge of her seat as the Movietone News came on. They were showing the British troops in Africa, and the audience cheered as they chased after a trundling German tank. Sophie studied each of the distant sunburned faces, some smiling and some serious, staring right into the camera lens. Dad was in Egypt – well, maybe he was there. She wasn't really certain where he was at this point. She silently urged the camera to move down among the mass of men watching a plane land, but instead it focused on the plane and its spinning propellors.

The feature film was *Goodbye Mister Chips*, starring Robert Donat. Sophie sank back into her seat, losing herself in the world of Mr Chips, the ageing schoolmaster.

About mid-way through the film the siren wail began, and an 'Oh!' of disappointment and resignation went up from the packed cinema as the lights came on.

Aunt Jessie followed the rest of the crowd to the exit, with Hugh held firmly by the hand. They all headed across the road to a large Underground station which was being used as a shelter.

The heavy rumbling drone of planes filled the sky and it was clear that the bombers were almost overhead. Sophie's heart was racing, though her legs felt almost too heavy to walk, let alone run.

The mad scramble down the steps became more frantic as she tried to follow her aunt, pushing her way along. There was a dreadful stench in the place – of stale urine and scared people. In a few minutes they would get used to it.

The huge tiled tunnel seemed to rumble.

'A hit! A direct hit!' the call went up.

Two hours later, the All Clear sounded, and they were able to make their way back to street level.

The Odeon was engulfed in flames that roared and lit up the dark of the evening sky. Firefighters surrounded it. Aunt Jessie stood, stock still, watching them. Grey-black smuts clung to her cheek, and her mascara and eye make-up had streaked and blotched, as big tears slid down her face. She gripped her niece and nephew tightly.

Sophie felt a strange shiver run down her spine as they watched the roof of the cinema collapse; the flaming curl of the metal seats on the balcony became visible for only an instant, before crashing down on the floor below.

They were lucky. Next time they might not be.

'That was too close,' whispered their aunt, 'much too close for comfort! I owe it to Libby to get you away from this. No more dilly-dallying. My mind's made up. You're going to Ireland tomorrow.'

CHAPTER 8

Farewell

'It's for the best,' Mum whispered weakly. She looked a bit better. 'He's a good man, your grandfather, do what he tells you and don't cause any trouble.'

'We'll be fine, we promise!' Sophie tried to sound cheerful.

Hugh was sitting on the edge of the bed, holding Mum's hand like he was never going to let it go.

'I'll be back on my feet in no time, back to my old self,' their mother tried to inject a note of optimism and confidence into her voice, 'then I'll come and get you.'

'Yes!' Sophie agreed.

But the blue eyes were already tired.

Nurse Harvey interrupted them. 'Mrs Stokes is waiting for you both. Come on! Give your Mum a big hug and a goodbye kiss,' she coaxed them.

Sophie wished that her mother was stronger, and could tell her about their grandfather and Ireland and give them some clue about what to expect.

Hugh was being brave, as brave as a seven-year-old who had lost his home could be. He buried his face in Mum's nightie, then stood up stiffly, like a small wooden puppet, and made space for Sophie. She wanted to hug Mum so tightly, but instead she held her gently, taking in the smell of lemon shampoo, and the faint hint of talcum powder that clung to Mum's skin. She closed her eyes, locking every detail of her mother's face into her memory.

Nurse Harvey coughed. Her eyes were blotchy red.

'Come on, Hugh!' Sophie caught hold of his hand. 'I'll take good care of him, Mum, I promise!'

Her mother nodded. Soon she would sleep. Sophie kissed her forehead, then turned away, pulling Hugh after her. She wanted this misery to end. Mrs Stokes was at the window, waiting. They had to go. Without any fuss they left.

Despite the early hour there was already a queue outside Bury Street centre, gangs of kids with nervous mums and dads. Cases and holdalls and sacks and bags littered the pavement. Mrs Stokes hurried Sophie and Hugh inside to get their stuff.

They had a small battered red case and a pillowcase tied with a piece of white string. Aunt Jessie had gone to their house and persuaded Mr Thompson, the street warden, to get them a few things. Some clothes, the photo of Dad in his uniform taken the day before he went away, an extra pair of shoes for Sophie. They each had a cardboard box holding their gas-mask hanging across their chest, and Mrs Stokes made them both put on their coats, as it was easier than carrying them. She took out a string and label and wrote Hugh's name and destination and where he was coming from, and attached it to the toggle of his coat. She took one look at Sophie's face and guessed, correctly, that the twelve-year-old would object loudly to being labeled like a paper package, and shoved the card and string back into her pocket.

'All set?' asked Mrs Stokes kindly.

Sophie nodded. The line outside was beginning to move. Some of the mothers were walking along beside their children, others stood with tears streaming down their faces as the children began the walk to the station. Everyone was trying to be cheerful, but no one was succeeding.

'Hugh! You've got to stick with me, we can't get separated, understand?' Sophie warned him. She was a bit worried. Hugh's freckles were standing out, and he had gone a shiny, whitish colour. He was over-excited and over-anxious.

In her mind Sophie tried to pretend that this was just like going on a school outing, or like the time she went with the school choir to Brighton to take part in a concert.

The huge station was in bedlam, with hundreds of children waiting there already. Most of them were clinging to their mums and dads, others were shoving and pushing, and some stood absolutely still, pretending, like Sophie, that this was not really happening, waiting to wake up, or for a grown-up to come to the rescue.

'Train to Wales! Train to Wales!' the station guard was shouting above all the racket.

Sophie knew she had to snap out of it – stop dreaming, stop pretending. 'Come on, Hugh! We want to get a good spot.' She wanted to get a window seat, so at least she could see where they were going. She had a purse with some money in it hanging from a string around her neck, inside her vest.

She wasn't taking any chances, as some of the other kids might be pick-pockets.

Volunteers from the Women's Voluntary Service had sheets of names, and were grouping about twenty kids at a time, then putting them up onto the dusty, black train. 'This is your seat, your seat for the entire journey. No running about and changing places. Mind you remember that!' they advised everyone.

There was crying and shouting and wailing and fighting as kids clung to parents, and babies bawled. Some people were putting their children on the train, and then, a few minutes later, lifting them off again, unable to let them go. The lists were going to be all muddled up at this rate, thought Sophie.

'Come on, Hugh! Up you get!' she shouted as she whooshed her brother and their load up from the platform and onto the train. From the doorway Sophie scanned the crowd, hoping that maybe Aunt Jessie might show up, but she had had to get back down to Kent, and was probably knee-deep in some kind of farm work at this very minute.

They sat silently in the carriage as the seats around them filled up. The woman across from them was red-eyed and kept blowing her nose as she held on to a plump little baby boy, all kitted out in blue wool, and a wide-eyed three-year-old who was waving to the dark-haired man in uniform standing outside the carriage window.

Sophie closed her eyes, blocking it all out, singing so softly to herself that only Hugh could hear.

CHAPTER 9

The Evacuees

The train was delayed because of all the confusion, but eventually it pulled out of Euston station with its cargo of evacuees. A loud cheer went up – Hurrah! Lots of the other children seemed to be delighted about leaving London and seemed to think that being evacuated was like going on some sort of holiday.

Their carriage, like all the others, was jammed with children of every shape, size and age. A girl about Sophie's age pushed in beside them with her younger brother and sister, shoving their luggage in the rack above and on the floor below them.

'Stop that crying, Lily! Do you hear me?' she ordered.

Big dirty tears ran down the little girl's face and she looked so miserable Sophie felt pity for her. The older girl turned and glared at Sophie, daring her to interfere.

Instead, Sophie stared out the window, watching the blur of back gardens and houses that sped by. She could see kitchen after kitchen, privies, lean-to's, rows of houses that clung haphazardly together, some bombed out and now deserted. Glimpses of streets with children playing, and row upon row of allotments, bursting with every kind of vegetable – no piece of ground could be wasted with the war on – and men and women digging and working. They were all doing their bit for the war effort, part of the 'home front', as Mr Churchill called it.

'Look at them 'lotments, Lily and Tom!' said the girl opposite. Both children craned for a better view.

Hugh was fascinated too. It was like a strange picture show, where you could see little bits and pieces of other people's lives. 'There's a scarecrow!' he called out.

'There's another one,' the other boy, Tom, added.

In a few minutes the three younger children had begun to point out things to each other.

The city had been left far behind and the open green countryside beckoned.

'A cow!' mouthed Lily. The older girl looked embarrassed. 'Maggie! I saw a cow, with its milk titties and all!' the little girl insisted.

Maggie blushed beetroot red as she knew that Sophie and the woman across from them had overheard.

'Plenty of them where we're going, our Lily, so you'd best get used to them,' she replied.

Sophie smiled.

'You going to Wales too?' the girl enquired.

'Well, sort of,' said Sophie. 'Actually, from there we're going to Ireland.'

'Ireland?' gasped Tom.

'Don't be letting me down, you two!' warned Maggie, 'you've seen Ireland on your maps in school.'

'It's an island!' they both chorused.

'They ain't havin' nuffin' to do with the war,' added Tom.

'They're neutral,' murmured Hugh.

There was an awkward silence, and the train seemed to be getting faster and faster.

'Why were you evacuated?' asked Maggie.

'We were bombed out, and our house is unsafe. Our Mum got injured.'

'Oooh! I'm sorry,' Maggie replied.

'She's in hospital, but she's going to get better, so Hugh and I are being sent off to stay with our grandfather in Ireland, as there's no one to take care of us,' said Sophie.

'We never ever saw him in our whole lives,' confided Hugh.

'You poor things!' consoled Maggie.

'What about the three of you?' Sophie asked, curious.

'Oh, we've just been sent out of London for safety. Our Mam is working in a munitions factory, alongside our big sister Sadie, and our brother Charlie is off fighting in Italy, and Len is kept busy helping, boarding up buildings and the like. Mam says that there's too much responsibility for a woman on her own, so we're being sent out of harm's way.'

Maggie opened up a package with thick wads of bread and jam which she shared out with Tom and Lily. Sophie had two slices of bread and dripping, and a small lemon curd tart, which Aunt Jessie had bought for her. It had gone a bit stale and the pastry had hardened. She gave Hugh a small drink of lemon barley from the bottle Mrs Stokes had given them. He gulped it down too quickly.

'Don't drink so much!' she warned, a little annoyed.

'But I'm thirsty, Soph!' he moaned.

She was thirsty herself, but only took a small dainty sip.

They had been well warned about not eating or drinking too much because of the shortage of toilets – and what would happen if about two hundred children needed to go at the same time! Didn't bear thinking about!

One of the lady escorts poked her head around the carriage door, checking on them. 'You lot okay? No one sick or anything?'

They all shook their heads. 'No!'

'Well! I'll pop by to see you again later,' she promised as she headed off down the train.

Sophie wished that all the signposts and station names hadn't been taken down, because at least then she would have a better idea where they were going and which towns and villages they were passing through.

They went into a long tunnel and everyone shrieked until a blue light came on. Then they travelled through beautiful fields and valleys. They passed two trains crowded with soldiers in uniform, which made everyone cheer. The five children chatted, mostly about home, and Sophie began to realise just how much she was going to miss it all.

For a while they all dozed and then Sophie woke to discover Hugh and Tom running up and down the train.

'Get back inside and sit down,' she ordered. She wished that Hugh and she were staying in Wales like Maggie and the rest.

Now the train was beginning to slow down. The countryside was rougher and more hilly. Wisps of smoke swirled up from grey stone houses and from cottages where mounds of dust and coal were stacked together, forming steep dark hills.

'We're here!' a chant ran up the train. 'Wales!'

'Is this it?' Hugh and his new friend both asked at the same time.

'Afraid so!' sniffed Maggie.

'Nobody move yet!' The order came from the lady escort. The train was going so slow it was almost shuddering. The escort came and sat down with them all for a minute. First she checked off their names from the list.

'Have you got everything?' she asked Maggie.

The girl nodded. She looked suddenly tired and tense.

'Now don't be worried or afraid, there's accommodation arranged for everyone. The billeting officer, Mrs Hughes, has it all set up and most of you will meet your families today and get settled in straight away,' she tried to reassure them.

'We're not staying in Wales!' Sophie told her.

For a second the woman looked puzzled.

'Sophie and Hugh Fitzpatrick,' Sophie said.

'Ah yes! Here you are! The two of you are going on the mail-boat from Holyhead to Ireland. You'll have to stay on the train a little longer. It's the next stop, I believe. Anyway, one of us will go with you. I'll be back to let you know,' she promised. 'Now, Maggie, you get ready to leave the train. Our assembly point is outside the station. About three hundred yards up the road there's a school – that's where we're heading. It's the reception centre.'

Maggie began to get her battered suitcase down from the overhead rack and Tom dragged the dirty pillowcase, crammed with grubby clothes, up on to his shoulder.

Sophie bit her lip.

Maggie was busy organising the smaller ones and bossing them about. 'Now don't cry, Lily! You just be good and polite, our Tom! We want to get a nice place to stay, so none of your antics, or you'll have to answer to me,' she warned.

Lily was so tired, she kept on yawning.

'Come on, you two!' Maggie scolded. Suddenly she stopped and turned back to Sophie.

'Best of luck in Ireland!'

'Best of luck to all of you!' replied Sophie. 'I hope you like your billet.'

'We'd better!' insisted Maggie.

They pushed out of the carriage and joined the throng of kids in the corridor jostling to get down off the train.

A huge crowd surged on to the platform. The very air was electric with excitement as they all talked and laughed and massed together.

Sophie wished she was going with them.

'Get in line! Get in line!' ordered the woman from the Women's Voluntary Service.

The volunteers and porters and station master were busy trying to organise them all and talking to those who were feeling lonely and afraid, as they began to file through the station.

Sophie searched the jumble of faces. There they were – Maggie with her ill-fitting clothes and wavy brown hair, Tom with the pillowcase trying to keep up with her, and little Lily sucking her thumb. All getting lost in the crowd.

As if by magic, Maggie turned and gave her a huge wave. They'd be fine! Sophie could tell by the way Maggie had stuck out her chin, and made herself taller and older-looking.

The whistle blew and jets of steam covered the windows, as the train began to chug again.

One of the volunteers almost flung herself into the empty seat beside them.

'I'm Judy Murray. Call me Judy,' she introduced herself, 'and I'm to get you to the mail-boat, safe and sound.'

Sophie and Hugh barely spoke. They watched the last of the evacuees disappear from view as they pulled out of the station.

CHAPTER 10

Run, Rabbit, Run

Hugh was watching Sophie. He was fretting about something, she could tell by the way he was shifting in the seat and fidgeting with his fingers.

'Sophie!'

'Hmm!'

'Sophie, are we cowards?' he whispered. She blinked. What in heaven's name was he talking about? 'Tom said we're running away to a country that won't help in the war.'

'Don't mind him!' she replied. But she could tell that this was not enough to satisfy him. 'Listen, Hugh! Maggie, Tom and Lily, and thousands just like them, just like us, are being evacuated for safety's sake. Mr Churchill and the Government have enough to worry about trying to stop Britain being invaded and all those German bombers that fly in night after night over London and all the other cities. They don't want to have to worry about us kids running around the place, getting hurt or lost or scared, so they reckon we're better off in the countryside, and it's easier to get food there.' Sophie stopped and thought. 'And in our case, it's just that we are being evacuated that bit further than the rest of them. We have a relation in Ireland, so it makes sense that we have to stay with him.'

'I s'pose so!' Hugh said quietly.

'Some children are going to America and Canada and Australia, Hugh! That's really far, oceans away. At least Ireland's only across the sea from England. It's not that far.'

'I s'pose so, but it still feels like we're running away, cowardy custards, like Tom said,' he kept on.

'Then in that case, we are just like all the others!' Sophie added adamantly.

She looked out the window. Two small brown rabbits were hopping and running and zig-zagging through the field outside, the noise of the train giving them a right old fright. Hugh caught sight of them too for a second before they disappeared into the safety of a hedgerow.

The rabbits were right to run from the train – it was too big, too noisy, too scary, something a rabbit could not possibly understand. Just like this war. Sophie knew that deep inside her she did not feel a coward. If anything, she was trying to be brave, the bravest she had ever, ever been.

Sophie began to sing softly,

'Run rabbit, run rabbit, run run run ...'

Hugh joined in the familiar song. She squeezed his hand. They were both being brave. Hugh's grey-blue eyes welled up with tears, but he seemed to understand. They both sang out, as the train rumbled on to Holyhead,

'Run rabbit, run rabbit, run run run ...'

CHAPTER 11

Sail Away

By the end of the five-hour journey they were both exhausted, and were pleased to stumble off the train and up to the Station Hotel, where Judy Murray organised tea and sandwiches. The hotel was packed with travellers, but Sophie was glad of the chance to use the bathroom, and to wash her grimy hands and face. Hugh wolfed down the dainty triangular-cut sandwiches.

'I'm starving!' he said, working his way through the whole plateful, and ignoring Sophie's warning kicks to his shins.

'Always nice to see a good appetite,' beamed their minder. 'It's the children who don't eat that I worry about.'

Sophie blushed. She was hungry, but at that moment the food tasted like sawdust in her mouth, and her stomach clenched up every now and then.

At last, Miss Murray escorted them down to the jetty where the huge mail-boat was waiting. It was the biggest ship Sophie had ever seen, much larger than any of the boats you'd see going up and down the Thames. It had two giant golden-coloured funnels that stuck up into the sky, and crowds of people were moving around the decks and leaning over the ship's side.

Sophie had never expected so many people to be going to Ireland at the same time, and they had to wait in line until it came to their turn to board, and cross over the wide gangplank, on to the slightly swaying deck.

Judy handed them over to the steward. He shook hands with both of them.

'Bill Cox,' he said. 'Now, I'm in charge of you while you're on this ship, so no chasing about or running around, no going places that are off-limits.' He took down their names on a page in a small notebook he kept in his uniform shirt pocket.

'What's down that way?' quizzed Hugh.

'Those are the cabins – you're not to go down there. Now, say goodbye to Miss Murray, and we'd best get a move on, as it looks like we've a full load on board today.'

Judy Murray shook hands with them solemnly and wished them luck, before disappearing into the crowd. Sophie suddenly realised just how much on their own they were now.

'All passengers aboard! All passengers aboard!' An announcement came through the loudspeaker and sent a shiver of excitement through the multitude of people pushing to look out over the rails as the massive engines began to judder and surge into life and a wash of churning water developed between them and land.

'Follow me!' ordered Mr Cox, briskly leading them to a busy lounge filled with wooden seats and benches.

They plonked down, shoving their cases underneath, and using the stuffed pillowcase like a bolster to lean against.

'I've a few jobs to attend to, so you're to sit right there! I'll be back as soon as I can,' their escort said.

All the seats began to fill up. Sophie watched their fellow

travellers out of the corner of her eye. The rest of them were all excited and happy about going to Ireland.

'It's good to be going home!' someone said.

'First time back to the old country in two years!' answered another.

'My mother said I was to come back and not risk getting blown to bits by the Germans!' answered a happy-looking young woman.

Some had such strong accents that Sophie could hardly make out a word they were saying. They all seemed to be laden down with cases and brown paper packages tied up in strange, curious shapes.

The ship was turning, swinging outwards. Everyone suddenly made a lunge towards the lounge door, shoving towards the open deck. The two children followed them. They were all waving themselves silly. It was so stupid, but Sophie and Hugh copied them as the mail-boat sailed away from Holyhead and the Anglesea coast.

'Hugh! We'd better get back inside in case Mr Cox is looking for us!' said Sophie after a few minutes.

'No! Please, Sophie, can't we stay out here?'

Sophie looked at her young brother. He was strangely pale and clammy. He was inhaling deep gulps of air and swallowing them down in an effort to make himself feel better.

Sophie felt fine and leant against the rail watching the people promenade past. The air around her was salty and damp, and her face felt moist with the sea-spray.

The ship was slowly and sluggishly turning away from the

Welsh coast, pushing out into the choppy Irish sea.

There were other children on board, but most of them were with adults. Two or three boys paraded past Sophie in school uniforms, heads together, talking in upper-class twit accents.

'I say, old fellah!' Sophie shouted into the wind.

The three of them turned around, puzzled for an instant, but seeing only herself and Hugh, who was by now feeling very sorry for himself, shrugged their shoulders, and moved on.

'Soph! Soph! I feel sick!' Almost as he said it, Hugh threw up. Most of it went over the ship's side but a bit clung ominously to the rail and deck. Sophie fumbled up her sleeve and in her knicker leg – she definitely had a handkerchief somewhere.

'It's all right, Hugh! Here you are!' She held it out to him.

He took it and tried to wipe himself. But the hanky was not much good, as he got violently seasick again, and again. In the end he slumped down on one of the wooden deck-chairs. 'I feel awful!' he sniffed, 'why did we have to go on this stinky old ship?'

'I know, Hugh! I know!' was all she could say.

At this stage the swell and the rocking motion of the waves were beginning to affect more of the passengers, and green- and grey-faced adults clung to the rails of the boat, sucking in the fresh air as if their very lives depended on it. Others just chatted away and enjoyed themselves. Sophie hoped that she had a strong stomach, as it would be disastrous if they were both sick.

Hugh looked exhausted but he had stopped retching. His stomach must surely be empty by now, Sophie thought.

'Come on, Hugh! Let's get you to the toilet.'

They walked through the lounge where the smell of sick clung in the air. It was crowded in the Ladies, with a long queue for the toilets. The basins were filthy, and there was so much water on the floor that it seeped through the sole of Sophie's shoe.

She made Hugh pull off his stained jumper and she rinsed out the grotty, disgusting hanky. She dabbed at the yellowish stains on his shirt and on the knees of his trousers. Hugh was too ill to protest.

'Throw water on your face!' she said bossily. 'Take a mouthful of water, and rinse out your mouth!'

She pulled down the grubby length of the roller towel, searching for a dry, clean bit, but it was no use. Finally they abandoned the hubbub of ladies and escaped outside.

Mr Cox was standing in the lounge, his squirrel-like brown eyes searching for them. Taking in Hugh's state in an instant, the steward pulled a spare label from his pocket, wrote Hugh's name again and pinned it anew to the small boy's shirt.

'Spring tides, that's what does it,' he told them. 'It's been like this all week, every crossing.'

Sophie nodded.

'I think you and your brother would be best out on deck. You go and get a place and I'll be back to you both in a few ticks.'

Two old men were sitting, chatting, and did not want to make space for two children, but Sophie ignored their frosty glances and shoved in near them. Poor Hugh felt too awful to care about anything.

Mr Cox came back with a loose, throw-over rug, which he tucked around Hugh. He also had a glass of fizzy water, and he handed it to the sick little boy. 'It's soda water – best thing to settle the stomach, young man!'

He held out a shiny metal bowl to Sophie in case of emergencies, and tossed her a tiny packet of dry biscuits. 'Just nibble those, they're meant to be good for nausea,' he said kindly.

'Thank you, Mr Cox,' said Sophie, but he had already headed off towards another passenger.

Hugh closed his eyes. Sophie knew that he was pretending to be someplace else – it was a game they played when they were scared or sick or bored. From the way he was pointing his fingers, she knew he was a cowboy, this time. Maybe riding a horse, and galloping across the prairies.

She shut her own eyes, but nothing happened. Sometimes, she would be a beautiful princess in a castle, or a Hollywood movie star. But right now she couldn't imagine anything nice. Maybe she was getting too old for the game. She was too conscious of the sea, and the ship and all the things that were taking her away from England, from Mum, and from her friends and neighbours and even her old school. The war – that was the cause of it all, and that Adolf Hitler wanting to run the whole of Europe! They'd all said it wouldn't last long.

But the Germans were spreading bit by bit into every country. What was to stop them invading Britain? Mr Churchill said that they would fight them everywhere – on the beaches, in the skies. She liked Mr Churchill. She trusted him.

Every night her mother would listen to the BBC, shushing herself and Hugh. She should have paid more attention to what was going on, realised how important it all was. Now she would have to try and make sense of it. This horrible, horrible war.

Hugh dozed, and Sophie tiptoed to the rail, staring into the churning waves below. The ship had to zig-zag, and change course, in case of any mines or u-boats in the shipping lane. It gave her goosebumps to think of a lumpy bit of metal bobbing under the water, just waiting ...

Hugh moaned, and tossed and sat up, grabbing at the metal bowl. Oh no! Not again!

The rest of the journey seemed to take an age. Hugh kept asking, 'Are we near land yet?' his voice anxious. 'Do you think there are any mines?'

Sophie did her best to banish thoughts of danger from his mind. 'Almost there! I wonder what it will be like? Aunt Jessie said Grandfather lives by the sea ...' She kept on trying to calm him, to get him to think of something other than this boat and the sea, rising and falling, and then, without her noticing, the blue-green smudge in the distance began to take shape. The blur got bigger and bigger – soon it was like a hill, then a mountain, then cliffs that stuck out into the blue of the sea. Ireland. Her very first glimpse. Sophie could hardly wait to land. 'Look, Hugh,' she said. 'There it is.' But there was no response. She looked down. Hugh definitely needed another trip to the Ladies. She bundled him through the crowds sprawled all over the passenger lounge. Babies lay spread-eagled, asleep on top of their mothers, and people were trying to tidy themselves up before they arrived at the harbour of Dun Laoghaire.

From afar it looked a nice town, church spires and pastel-painted houses. In the distance she could see the long stretch of coastline, and wondered where was Greystones, the place her grandfather lived.

'Come on, Hugh!' she ordered, impatient now.

He still looked peaky and sick. She wanted him to look healthy and well – and clean – when they met their grandfather. She did not want Grandfather to think they were the type of children that would be troublesome.

Inside, her own stomach was churning, not with seasickness, but with nerves. What if Grandfather didn't like them, or they didn't like him?

'Sophie!' Mr Cox's voice interrupted. 'You and your brother are to wait till the end to disembark. I want to make sure there's someone here to meet you.'

Sophie simply nodded, too scared to speak. She stifled a yawn and suddenly realised just how tired she was after the long journey.

The two arms of the long grey stone piers opened out into the sea as if welcoming them, and the mail-boat sailed into the very middle of the wide embrace. A necklace of pink and white and pale blue and yellow terraced houses lined the charming seafront, with the town rising up behind them.

Soon all movement ceased and the big bulk of their boat came to rest against a pier. As soon as the large gangplank went over, people began to swarm across.

They had finally arrived. They were in Ireland, their new home.

CHAPTER 12

The Welcome

Sophie watched as families were reunited. They hugged and kissed and talked animatedly to each other. Some solitary figures stood, holding their cases, looking forlorn. The schoolboys were met by a plump woman in a fur coat who hugged and kissed them all, much to their embarrassment.

'Come on, children!' Mr Cox urged, leading Sophie and Hugh down the gangplank. He carried their case, but Sophie kept hold of the pillowcase, and slung it over her shoulder. The steward dealt with the two passport inspectors in dark uniforms, then led them to the sunlit exit from the port. People were everywhere, standing, sitting, watching, waiting. Sophie hoped that their grandfather was amongst them. Mr Cox chatted away to them, all the time with his eyes scouring the crowd. At one stage, he left them and approached a balding, jolly-looking gentleman who seemed to be asking one of the ship's officers something. He seemed friendly, just as Sophie imagined a grandfather should be. But she could see him shake his head.

'Where is he?' complained Hugh, voicing her own concerns. 'He's probably forgotten and won't bother coming to get us.'

'He will, Hugh! Aunt Jessie and Mrs Stokes both told us he would!' said Sophie, conscious of the knot of fear that sat like a toad in her stomach.

Then she noticed the tall man sitting on one of the wooden benches reading a newspaper. As if he knew she had spotted him, he folded the paper and began to stand up. He had a grey beard and a broad face, which even at a distance reminded her of her own father. He was wearing a blue-green tweed suit and a white shirt, and as soon as he walked she couldn't help but notice his pronounced limp, and the gnarled dark wooden stick he used.

Mr Cox spotted him too and began to nudge them in his direction.

'Do you think that's him?' whispered Hugh.

Sophie shrugged.

'Excuse me, Sir! Are you, by any chance, Professor Fitzpatrick?' Mr Cox enquired.

The old man looked sternly at them. 'Yes! Indeed I am! And these two must be my grandchildren, Sophie and Hugh!' He gave a kind of low, formal bow, and instead of hugging them shook their hands politely.

Sophie wilted from his stare – the striking pale blue eyes under the grey hairy eyebrows gazed at her.

Then she stared straight back at him, taking in the reddish veins that criss-crossed his cheeks and the few stray hairs that lurked in the shadows of his nose, and the frown that creased his brow. And then, his eyes. His gaze was cold and distant.

He turned his attention to Hugh, and Sophie could almost see the disappointment as he took in the pale, sick little boy with grey shadows under his eyes, and the still slightly stained shirt and jumper and trousers.

'He was sick, Grandfather!' Sophie tried to explain, wishing that they had made a better first impression.

The old man just nodded and turned to Mr Cox. Sophie watched as her grandfather slipped the steward a tip. 'Thank you, my good man, for seeing this precious cargo safely home,' he said. 'I wonder if you could do us one more favour and organise having this luggage' – he pointed to the worn case and the now dirty pillowcase – 'transferred to the station, as we are taking the next train to Bray.'

'Very well, Sir!' Mr Cox agreed.

'I can carry it, Grandfather,' Sophie blurted out.

'You can, but you may not, Sophie! Mr Cox will see to it,' he ordered firmly.

Their grandfather turned around and began to walk towards the station. Sophie and Hugh followed him. He was used to giving orders, Sophie could see, and to having people follow him. That was the kind of man he was.

The station was busy, and as soon as the train came there was a surge forward to find a carriage. Grandfather did not speak to them again until they were actually sitting on the train.

'You must both be very tired!' he offered. He seemed bored by their company already.

Hugh yawned in affirmation. Sophie felt tears prick her eyes and she just about managed to nod. She stared out the train window as it trundled along through a wake of breathtaking scenery – and the sea was always there, blue and sparkling and winking at her. There were cliffs and hills that tumbled down to the coast and beach below, and tunnels cutting through them as the railway track seemed to hover right to the edge. Large houses clung to the hillsides, with gardens surounded by flowers and shrubs.

'It's so beautiful!' she gasped. Certainly it was not what she had expected.

'Yes,' said her grandfather proudly. 'This is Killiney – they call it the Naples of Ireland. I suppose they are a bit alike.'

'When will we be there?' asked Hugh. Although he was cuddled up beside her, Sophie could see him every now and then sneaking looks at this strange new grandfather.

'Not too long now, young man!' Grandfather promised.

They passed a long stony beach, where dogs were being walked by their owners.

Before they knew it, the train had come to a halt at Bray, a seaside holiday town, where they had to get off. They followed again as their grandfather pushed through the heavy metal turnstile out to the station exit.

'Ah! There you are, Edward!' he said as they came onto the road.

Sophie and Hugh could not believe it – a horse and trap stood outside the station waiting for them! The big brown horse blinked and turned his head towards them.

'Up you get, young Miss!' The driver, Mr Devins, was a smallish man, wearing a brown cap and jacket; his face was tanned, and wore an amused expression as he helped Sophie to step up into the trap. She sat on one side, and her grandfather positioned himself opposite, one leg sticking forward stiffly. Hugh was all excited. He had never been in a trap before. Wide awake now, he squeezed up on the bench beside Sophie. Mr Devins placed a warm rug over their knees, and stored their case away on a metal rack, then climbed up into the front of the trap, caught hold of the dark-brown leather reins, and made a clicking sound with his mouth. The horse seemed to lift up his ears, then began to move forward at the command, and went clip clop up along the street.

Bray was a busy town, and they passed many shops and houses before eventually getting out on the open road.

'This is the road to Greystones,' their Grandfather announced. 'Those are the Sugarloaf mountains, the big Sugarloaf and the little one.' He pointed to the large mountain, with its crust of grey-and-white, like icing covering the top.

Grey stone walls gave way to green fields, dotted with cows and sheep, then the road began to climb a bit and Sophie could tell it was hard going for the horse.

'I'll walk for a while, Mr Devins!' she offered, to make the load lighter. And she walked alongside the driver who had got down himself.

'She's a good horse, is Sheba!' said Mr Devins gently.

'She's lovely!' said Sophie, patting the horse's smooth neck.

Once they cleared the hill, Sophie clambered back in.

'I see the sea!' declared Hugh, as patches of blue sneaked through the spring hedgerows. Down below, the little town of Greystones clustered beneath them.

The horse walked slowly so as to be sure not to slip.

It was immediately clear why the place was called Greystones. The waves rushed in on a beach made up completely of stones, of every shape and size and every shade of grey, from almost white to a shiny black.

'This is the North Beach,' Grandfather informed them. Fishing boats were pulled up on the beach and slipway. 'That's our pier.' Part of the pier seemed to have broken off, and must have fallen into the sea. 'A ship crashed into it, and then, bit by bit, storms and heavy seas did the rest.'

Mr Devins slowed Sheba down, so that they could have a good look at the place.

They rounded the seafront, and passed by a huge hotel. Over the hedges they could make out lawns and a croquet garden. Further along the road, a line of large imposing houses looked out to sea.

Sophie could scarcely believe it when Mr Devins turned the pony and trap into the driveway of one of these houses, and the horse trotted up to the front door.

'There you are, Professor! Right to your doorstep, safe and sound!' Mr Devins declared, jumping down to help them out.

'But it's huge, Grandfather!' gasped Hugh. 'Do you live here all by yourself?'

The old man seemed a bit embarrassed. 'Yes, Hugh, I do! But now that the two of you are here, well, there will be someone else around to fill up the place!'

Sophie couldn't make out if he was annoyed or pleased that they were there.

'Welcome to your new home,' said Grandfather formally.

CHAPTER 13

Carrigraun

'Come inside,' their grandfather ordered brusquely.

Mr Devins had left their luggage on the red-tiled porch, and Sophie felt rather nervous as he and Sheba turned and disappeared along the seafront, leaving them all alone with this strange new grandfather. But not for long.

'Nancy!' Grandfather called out. A cheerful-looking red-haired young woman appeared from the kitchen. 'Children! I'd like you to meet my housekeeper, Nancy. Nancy, this is Sophie and this is Hugh.'

'Well! I'm truly glad to meet you at last,' Nancy said. 'The professor has done nothing but talk about you both for the last few days! He's been right excited about you being evacuated to stay with him.' Her green eyes danced at the discomfiture of her employer, who turned away, embarrassed, and went off to the dining room.

Nancy chatted on excitedly. 'Bit of a change from London! You poor things, being bombed out and all that. We're lucky that Mr deValera kept us out of it! Doesn't bear thinking about!'

Nancy ushered them into the dining room for a light dinner of lamb chops and potatoes. They sat at a large old mahogany table, Grandfather at the top, eating his way slowly and silently through his meal. The children ate in silence too. Only

Nancy chatted and broke the tension. Finally, the old man pushed back his chair and got up from the table.

'Time for my evening walk. Nancy will show you to your rooms,' he said.

Sophie was disappointed that her grandfather had not wanted to talk to them, to hear about Mum and Dad, and their lives in London. He didn't seem to be at all interested, and she was too shy to ask the hundreds of questions that rattled around in her brain, demanding answers.

Sophie's room was big and the yellow brass bed was so tall she would have to climb up into it. Nancy had turned back the sheet and coverlet, and put in a hot-water bottle. It was very comforting. The room was decorated in a pale pink wallpaper with a deep pink stripe, and a line of trailing pink and blue flowers all around the top. The curtains were pink too, and hung from a thick bamboo-like curtain pole. Nancy closed over the curtains, blocking out the end of evening light. 'Into bed, Sophie,' she said. 'You need to sleep, child.'

Hugh's room was smaller and painted yellow and blue. His window overlooked the garden. He was in bed in seconds, too tired to protest.

Sophie tossed and turned for a while. The horsehair mattress at first seemed too hard, but finally she settled down, warm and comfortable. Here, lying in the dark, Sophie felt safe at last, in this room, in this house. No bombs, no sirens, no air-raid shelters, no swivelling beams of searchlights.

There was a knock on the door, then it creaked open. It was Hugh, in an old washed-out stripy pair of pyjamas. 'I can't sleep! I can't sleep, Soph! It's too quiet!'

Sophie almost giggled. He was right! It was so quiet and peaceful. All there was was the gentle shush of the waves outside, and a wobble of pale moonlight that gleamed through the curtain.

'Honest, Soph, I can't sleep!'

Sophie patted the narrow bed and her brother clambered in beside her, his bony knees and arms sticking into her. Out of habit, they both said their night-prayers, thinking specially of Mum and Dad, and adding their grandfather to the list of people to be prayed for.

In seconds, Hugh drifted off to sleep. Sophie lay awake. She was exhausted too, but her head was swimming with thoughts of this long, long day and all that had happened.

Lots of children were sleeping in strange beds tonight, she told herself – Maggie and her brother and little Lily, and all the others from the train. She and Hugh weren't the only ones feeling homesick and lonely.

It was all part of the war effort. You had to make the best of it, that's what everyone was expecting of you. She thought of Mum in the hospital and Dad in the war, and knew she must be brave for their sake.

Grandfather returned from his walk. She heard the heavy front door beneath her window bang shut. Would he come up to wish her goodnight, she wondered? But then she heard another door opening and closing. He wasn't going to come.

There was no point in comparing him with her mother's father, Grandad Joe. Sophie remembered him so well. He was fun and told stories and played games with her. She had always been his favourite, his special granddaughter. She had loved him so much, but he had died when Hugh was only three.

This grandfather was different. He was their flesh and blood too, but he had never come to London to visit them, or seen them when they were babies. He was stern and distant, and he just wasn't interested in them. No wonder Dad never talked about him. She couldn't help but think that it was a mistake to have come to Ireland, even if it was safe, but now there was no going back.

Before breakfast the next morning, Sophie unpacked the few bits of clothes they had and hung them in the two huge wardrobes in their bedrooms. She draped her spare dress and cardigan over the polished wooden hangers that swung from the central bar. Her clothes looked lost in the emptiness of the wardrobe. She put her few bits of underwear and stockings in one of the drawers in the large chest of drawers. She hoped Grandfather would not check and see how little they both had.

'You will both have the run of the house,' announced Grandfather at breakfast, 'with the exception of my study downstairs and my bedroom, dressing room and bathroom. I will point out those rooms to you after breakfast. I expect you to respect my privacy. The drawing room is not to be treated as a playroom. Meals are regular. Good wholesome nourishing food – you two need building up – served on time. Breakfast is at half-past eight, lunch at one o'clock, and tea is at half-past six. Nancy is used to these hours and they suit her.'

Hugh was shifting uncomfortably and Sophie could tell he was making an effort to try and remember all that Grandfather was saying.

'Lights are not to be left on unnecessarily, hot water is not to be wasted, and I will not tolerate loudness or unruly behaviour.'

'And now,' he continued, 'about your education. I will arrange for you to attend the local schools here from next Monday. You, Sophie, will go to the convent school, and you, Hugh, to the boys' school nearby.' He stopped talking for a few seconds as he cut the top off his egg and dropped a knob of butter into it. 'You may have this week off.'

Sophie was amazed at just how much food there was on the breakfast table: bread, butter, jams, marmalade, eggs, a big jug of milk, and a large silver teapot. Where was their grandfather getting it all from?

'Grandfather, do you have to get ration cards for us?' she blurted out.

'Don't worry about that, Sophie. Remember, the food shortages here are nothing as bad as in London – this is an agricultural country. I'll sort out the allowances for the two of you.'

She blushed. Every time he spoke to her, it was as if he was giving her a lecture.

'I suppose the pair of you are anxious to explore your new surroundings?' he continued. 'Now, listen carefully. No climbing the rocks – with the sea-spray they are too slippery at this time of year. Be careful of the tide if you go on the South Beach or Cove.'

South Beach! Cove! It sounded like there were lots of places to see, and Sophie was itching to get out and have a good look around.

'Sophie, you are responsible for your brother,' Grandfather said. 'Make sure he does not get into trouble – and be careful of the water.'

'Are you finished, Professor?' interrupted Nancy, starting to clear the table.

'I have some work to do,' said the old man. 'Bring me the post when it comes, Nancy.'

Sophie thought he had forgotten about herself and Hugh, but he looked at the two of them again. 'I trust you two will be able to amuse yourselves till lunchtime? Now, come with me.'

He pointed out the doors to his private rooms, then opened the last one into a room filled with books. He limped inside and closed the door behind him.

CHAPTER 14

Greystones

Greystones – Sophie had only been in the place a few hours, but she loved it already, and as for Grandfather's house, never, ever did she dream of staying in such a fine billet.

The house was called Carrigraun, and it stood like a huge grey sentry keeping guard over the sea-front, watching the fishing boats go in and out, and the passing of distant ships, from its huge bay-windowed glass eyes. In places, bits of paint were peeling, a result of winter storms and the salt-edged sea breeze that was carried over the waves.

Just imagine, living in a house near two beaches, mused Sophie. In fact, there were three, if you counted the rocky Cove with its rock pools and little caves.

South Beach was totally different from the other beach which disappeared in a beige, sandy line in the distance. Here it was shingly and covered in tiny stones of every imaginable colour. They both took off their shoes and socks and waded into the water. The shifting shale and stones hurt their feet, making them wince with pain, and the freezing water swirled around their ankles, sending jabs of ice into their veins. Still, they hopped up and down with excitement, shouting, 'Ouch! Ouch!' as they paddled about.

The strand was deserted except for two fishermen wearing protective rain-clothes and funny tweed hats, who sat on two small stools holding their huge, tall rods, the lines cast far into the sea, as they waited patiently for a bite.

Sophie and Hugh watched and waited for ages, then, eventually bored, moved on. They used Hugh's socks to knock the stinging sand off their feet and dry them before putting their shoes back on.

They crossed under a railway bridge, and seeing shops in the distance, headed for the town. There was a white-painted library, with a big notice about the opening times, and Sophie hoped that Grandfather would agree to let her join it, as he was unlikely to have many books that a girl her age might read back in the house.

They rambled past the window displays and the enticing bustle of shopkeepers and customers. Today was a day for exploring, not for hanging around listening to local chit-chat and shop gossip, though the people seemed friendly, and a few of them smiled at the children.

Suddenly they heard a familiar clip-clop sound behind them in the street and they turned to see Mr Devins. He had two old ladies in the pony and trap and they drew up outside the station. He helped them down, then carried their luggage inside.

Sophie and Hugh were delighted to see a familiar face and decided to wait for him.

'Well! Well! If it isn't the two little war orphans!' he boomed out across the street.

'Mr Devins!' Sophie interrupted him crossly, 'we are not orphans!'

'I know that, Miss Fitzpatrick,' he apologised, 'it's more a figure of speech, a slip of the tongue. Now, tell me honestly, how are you both settling in? The professor hasn't starved you, or beaten you yet?'

'Honestly, Mr Devins!' protested Sophie, 'our grandfather would never do such a thing, he's a ...' she stopped, realising that she was defending a grandfather she barely knew.

Mr Devins was chuckling away to himself. 'Don't be getting yourself in a tizzy, lass, I was only pulling your leg. People around here have a lot of respect for the professor, a mighty lot of respect.'

Hugh, sensing his sister's embarrassment, decided to take a hand in the conversation. 'We went for a paddle on the South Beach! It was freezing cold.'

'Aye!' grunted Mr Devins. 'Best to wait till summer comes when there's donkeys and all on the beach. You'll be able to swim every day. Do you like swimming, the pair of you?'

Sophie pasted a bright, lying smile across her lips, and opened her brown eyes wide. She wasn't going to admit that neither she nor Hugh could swim a stroke. They had only ever been to the seaside twice before when she was younger – other than that there had just been the odd day-trip to Brighton. There had never been enough money for holidays. Her father could swim – any wonder, she thought, growing up in a place like this? He had promised that some day he would teach them, but it had never happened and Sophie was beginning to doubt that it ever would.

'Well, where are you two off to now?' Mr Devins asked.

'We were thinking of going down to the harbour,' she replied.

'Let you hop in then! I'm heading down that way myself.'

'Are you sure?'

'Lassie, I wouldn't offer otherwise. I'm going home for an hour, then I've to bring someone from Windgates into Bray. Funny old thing, this emergency! What with petrol being rationed, me and old Sheba are doing great business,' he confided.

The trap tilted and dipped as they stepped in, then off they trotted. Mr Devins gave them a running commentary on each house they passed, telling them who lived there and what they did, until a few minutes later he deposited them at the curved harbour.

There, the fishermen had nets spread over the railings and on the grey wall and the ground, and were busy mending them. A pile of lobster pots lay in a heap against a boathouse and Hugh nearly sent them all flying when he picked one up to look at it.

'Leave those pots alone!' shouted a cranky old fisherman.

They ran down the slope of beach and climbed among the boats lying there, sitting in them and pretending to row. Time seemed to fly by, there in a world of their own.

'I'm starving, Soph! When is it going to be lunchtime?' demanded Hugh finally.

Sophie leapt out of the boat. Oh no! The station clock had shown almost midday probably about an hour ago!

'Come on, Hugh! Run!'

They ran helter-skelter the whole way along the seafront and skidded along the gravel driveway of Carrigraun, both sweaty and out of breath. Through the window they could see their grandfather, sitting at the dinner table waiting for them.

Hugh's hands were filthy and Sophie had a smudge of tar on her dress.

'Quick, Hugh!' she said in a panic.

They washed their hands and brushed their hair and joined their grandfather.

He had finished his bowl of soup, and Nancy appeared immediately and plumped two steaming bowls of vegetable soup in front of them. It was scalding hot, and Sophie, knowing that the old man would be impatient for his main course, almost burnt her mouth trying to swallow it down. Hugh kept blowing across the top of his bowl and onto the curved silver spoon.

'Manners!' muttered Grandfather, but Hugh just ignored him, and kept on blowing.

'Grandfather! We're sorry. We didn't realise the time,' Sophie apologised.

'Hmmmph!' was his only reply.

He chose not to speak to either of them again until after their main course of salty ham and potatoes and broad beans and carrots.

'Well then! What did you think of the place?' he demanded suddenly.

Sophie considered. She wanted to be honest, and yet did

not want to be disloyal to Grove Avenue and London. 'It's very nice, Grandfather, and I would think that it's a very healthy place to live.'

He threw back his grey head and laughed, thumping his hand on the table. Under his whiskers, Sophie could make out a dimple. Had she sounded stupid, she wondered?

'I think it's spiffing – like a book,' said Hugh. 'But still, it's not as nice as home,' he added wistfully.

Grandfather stood up. 'Remember,' he stated, 'this is your home for the moment – while this war madness continues.'

CHAPTER 15

Hide and Seek

Over the next few days both of them ran wild, coming back to Carrigraun only to eat and sleep. Every morning Grandfather disappeared off into his study to work, and for the most part ignored them. They still had a few days left before starting school.

Nancy was kind to them and occasionally told them stories about the locals of Greystones. Sometimes Sophie felt like she was in a kind of a dream, a no man's land, where no one really minded what Hugh and herself, the two outsiders, were up to.

Then one day the rain lashed down and they had to stay indoors. Overnight the sea had become grey and menacing, the waves churning and battering against the rocks across from the house. It was like some ancient creature trying to cross a moat, flinging itself against the sea-front, dashing itself backwards and forwards, as yet another huge swell gathered force, far in the distance. Salt spray filled the air and overhead hung a black stormy sky. The whole of Greystones was wrapped in a blanket of mist which seemed to deny the existence of an outside world.

Sophie and Hugh had tried to venture out, but the wind had stolen their breath, driving them back, and the stinging rain had drenched them to the skin. Hugh looked like a very small drowned rat, and Sophie's hair clung like a damp cap to her skull.

Nancy scolded them sharply for being so stupid, and made them hang their saturated clothes near the big old range to dry. They both hunched up close to the fire, trying to dry themselves off with towels.

It was awful being forced to stay inside. Carrigraun seemed gloomy and dreary, like a prison from which they could not escape.

Grandfather was busy working in his study and would be annoyed if they disturbed him, so it was up to Sophie to keep Hugh quiet and out of harm's way.

Luckily she found a worn-out pack of cards and she sat down at the dining table to play with him, hoping he was too young to notice that the four and ace of clubs were missing, and that they only had two queens. He could only concentrate for about an hour or so, then he got restless.

'I'm bored!' he said.

'But you're winning!' she consoled him. It was a bit of a job, but she was doing her best to make sure he won most of the time.

'Bored with a capital B,' he said stubbornly. 'Let's play tag!'

'No, Hugh!' she replied.

'Then hide and seek – please Sophie! You can hide first!'

'Oh all right then. But not too much noise, do you hear!' she added, bored herself.

Sophie ran up the stairs, wondering which room to pick. In the end she settled for the large walk-in hot press. It was lined with shelves of towels, bed linen, and men's shirts and clothes. She would wedge her way into the deepest corner, and maybe drape a towel down to hide behind. It was very dark inside as only three small holes let light in from the outside, and she hoped that Hugh wouldn't take too long to discover her.

Hunkered down, she ran her hand along the slats of varnished wood. Someone had scratched something on one of the slats – maybe a name or a secret message?

There was no sign of Hugh, so she got back up and opened the door a fraction, letting in a shaft of light. She could read it now: NEIL – her father's name. It was carved out in deep, long straight lines. She pulled the door closed again. He must have hidden here too. It comforted her to think of him running around this house many years ago.

She could hear a step outside and got a terrible urge to giggle. The door was flung open. 'Got you!' screamed Hugh, all excited, as she emerged into the blinding light.

'Ssh! Ssh!' she warned him. 'Grandfather!'

They took turns all afternoon. Yelling and shouting with excitement when they got too close or found each other. Then Hugh was gone for ages and ages. Sophie searched upstairs and downstairs, under things, behind things, and still she could not find him.

Where in heaven's name had he got to? He wasn't in the garden as it was still pouring outside.

'Hugh! Hugh!' she called softly, beginning to get worried now. As if drawn by a magnet or some strange warning instinct, she tiptoed back upstairs and opened her grandfather's bedroom door.

There was a large double bed in the centre of the room, with a heavy sea-blue silk quilted cover on it. At one side of the bed a table almost toppled over with an uneven pile of books and a dusty old bedside light.

'Hugh! I hope you're not hiding in here,' she whispered.

She looked at the huge dark wardrobe; on one side of it was a doorway to what must be a dressing room.

'Hugh!' she pleaded urgently.

'Sophie, look!' Hugh almost jumped out from behind the dressing-room door. 'Look what I found!'

Sophie nearly died with fright – it was a leg, a wooden leg! Hugh was waving it around like it was a cricket bat.

'Stop it, Hugh! You might break it.'

'There's lots of them, look!'

Sophie swallowed hard when he swung open the cupboard door to reveal a collection of legs – some flesh-coloured, one white and gleaming, looking almost like bare bone, and two shaped to resemble a normal adult leg.

'Hugh! Come away!'

But her brother was over-excited, showing off. The legs must have scared the daylights out of him when he discovered them. Now he was getting his own back on her with his display of bravado.

'Don't touch them, Hugh!' she ordered, but he just ignored her.

He was pretending to limp around the room, lifting up one leg and trying to balance on the wooden leg. 'Arrgh my hearties! I'm a big bad pirate and I want your gold!' He paced up and down, getting more reckless.

Sophie couldn't calm him down. She turned back towards the bedroom just as the large looming figure of her grandfather appeared.

'What are you doing? How dare you invade my bedroom!' His eyes were cold and unflinching.

Sophie's face flamed with guilt. She should have made sure that Hugh hadn't come into this room. Hugh had managed to knock the rest of the legs out onto the floor, where they lay in a grotesque pile.

'What is this! What have you done?' roared their grandfather.

Hugh began to giggle – not the right thing to do at all as it made the old man angrier.

'Pick them up carefully and place them back where they belong!' he ordered stonily.

Hugh looked like some kind of octopus, with legs sticking out at every angle.

'One by one – carefully!'

'Grandfather, we ... we're sorry, honestly!' pleaded Sophie. 'We didn't mean to do any harm, it's just that it's so wet outside and we got bored, Hugh wanted to play. We didn't mean to touch your things ...'

'I told you both not to come into my room. Do you two understand English? You have plenty of places to go in this

90

house. I have accepted having the two of you foisted on me, but I am at least entitled to my own privacy in my own home.' He was shouting now.

Hugh was trying to look contrite. 'I never saw an artificial leg before, Grandfather,' he said. 'They're funny-looking things!'

Her grandfather raised his hand as if to hit the child but Sophie forced her way between them. 'Don't touch him!' she warned.

'You want to see what an artificial leg looks like? Then I'll show you!' Grandfather began to roll up his brown tweed trouser leg, exposing the pale painted shape that replaced the flesh and bone. There was a grotesque raised scar at the top, a bump of mottled skin like a line dividing the real from the unreal.

Horrified yet fascinated, the two children stared. Hugh's eyes were almost popping out of his head.

'Are you satisfied now, you young pup?' Grandfather demanded. He stood, almost swaying with emotion in front of them. 'Now get out of my sight, the two of you! Go to your rooms!'

They both ran off, relieved to get away from him. Sophie made sure that Hugh went into his own room despite his pleas to stay with her.

She flung herself on her bed, utterly miserable. She was so ashamed of their behaviour. They should never have gone into Grandfather's room – it was all their own fault. They had broken their promise and invaded his privacy. He must think that they were two very bad-mannered children. What if he wrote to their parents or the authorities to complain about them? Where would they be sent then?

Sophie knew that she couldn't leave things the way they were. Oh why did Hugh have to be so bold sometimes! If only he hadn't gone into the bedroom!

Grandfather probably thought they were jeering at him. His poor leg! She wondered what had happened to him. Maybe he had fought in a war like Dad was doing now. Still, he shouldn't have tried to hit Hugh, no matter how annoying he was. He was still small.

Nancy slipped a tea-tray wordlessly into her room, refusing to be drawn into conversation or forced to take sides.

Mrs Kellett, Sophie's teacher in her old school, had always said never to be afraid to apologise and say sorry. She said that it took backbone and good character always to do the right thing.

Sophie made up her mind what she would do. She marched up to her grandfather's study and knocked on the door.

CHAPTER 16

This Is London

'Who is it?' Grandfather called out irritably.

'It's me! Sophie!'

She could hear him moving around, shuffling papers, making up his mind whether to let her in or not.

'Oh! All right then! Enter!'

Sophie pushed the white-panelled door in. Her grandfather was sitting at a big old wooden desk, which was covered in papers and letters. Sophie's eyes travelled around the book-cluttered room. It was like a small library, with shelves reaching almost to the ceiling. It would take years to read all these books. No wonder Grandfather spent almost all his time in here. There was so much knowledge and learning just in this one place.

His half-eaten tea lay balanced on top of a pad of writing paper. Sophie almost tripped over a box on the floor.

'Mind my files!' he exclaimed. He had a pen in his hand and had obviously been writing. 'Let me finish the rest of this page.' He motioned to her to sit down. She sat in a smaller version of the green-winged leather chair he was sitting in, and watched as he wrote, muttering softly to himself.

Sophie's eyes suddenly noticed the high shelf of strange objects in glass jars. They shone with an incandescent dark green glow. What in heaven's name were they? Then she almost jumped out of her skin with fright when her eyes settled on the grimacing skull of a skeleton, hanging from a stand in the corner.

'Oh!' she screamed.

Her grandfather looked up. 'That's only old Toby! My skeleton. All us medical students used to have our own skeletons. No need to be scared of him.' He stood up and walked over to the bony figure. 'I'll cover it up if it upsets you.' He draped a heavy piece of brown velvet over it, then turned back towards her, stiffly.

'Well?' He drew his pipe and pouch of tobacco out of his pocket and began to fill the bowl.

'Grandfather, I'm sorry to interrupt you when you're working, but I wanted to come and apologise properly for what Hugh and I did. I know it was very wrong.'

He began to light the pipe, waiting for her to say more.

'We would never jeer or laugh at anyone because of a war injury, and we're sorry if we caused you any pain or upset. We appreciate very much what you're doing for us.'

He sucked in a draft of air as the pipe began to smoke. 'I'm not used to having children round this place,' he said at last. 'Perhaps it was a mistake. Maybe you'd have been better off evacuated to Wales –'

'But we love it here, Grandfather,' Sophie blurted out, 'we love Greystones.'

But he made no reply, and his stern eyes simply stared at her as he puffed on his pipe, making her feel small and uncomfortable.

'Anyway ... we ... we're sorry,' she mumbled.

'Hmph!' was his only response, which Sophie took to mean apology accepted. She didn't know whether to stay in the room now or leave. Already her grandfather seemed to have lost interest in her and was looking at the papers on his desk. Then on a sort of inlaid sideboard Sophie spotted it – a wireless! It was a bigger version of the one they had at home, but it had the same brown casing and the dials and buttons at the bottom. There were papers and books piled on top of it.

'A wireless!' she gasped.

Her grandfather looked up.

'Grandfather! Does the wireless work?' she asked.

He nodded.

'Can you receive the BBC on it?' She was excited now.

'Yes, of course I can, and the World Service too.'

'Oh please, Grandfather, could we listen?'

Sophie suddenly realised how far removed she felt from England and from the war effort. From everything that was going on at home. From the British army and navy and air force. From what Mr Churchill was saying. Just because she was in Ireland she shouldn't forget about them all.

Her grandfather looked at his watch. 'The nine o'clock news should start in a few minutes,' he said. 'Are you really interested in the *news*, Sophie?' he asked in surprise. He actually seemed curious about her now.

'We always listened at home. Mum always wanted to know how the troops were getting on,' said Sophie, 'in case there was any news of Dad and his unit.' Most of the time Sophie herself had only half-listened, in fact, but now it was an important link she longed for.

The wireless whirred as he turned it on, and voices in different languages and accents blurred together until he tuned it and the familiar voice of the English newsreader came reassuringly across the airwaves.

'This is the BBC London with the nine o'clock news.'

Sophie sat rigid and still, listening to the voice from home.

Her grandfather continued to write but listened too, every now and then making some comment about one of the politicians or leaders.

Sophie tried to concentrate her best on all that was being said. It was only at the end of the broadcast that she remembered Hugh. He was probably still awake, waiting to hear how she had got on.

She stood up to go. 'Thank you! May I come to listen again please?'

Grandfather simply nodded.

Sophie raced off to tell Hugh all about the wireless.

CHAPTER 17

Dolly and Maud

'Like two urchins! Running wild, that's what people are saying!' a strange voice in the hall announced.

'Two war orphans dressed in rags,' another voice added, slightly more hesitantly.

Sophie stared down over the bannisters on the landing. She could see the tops of two heads. There were two women standing in the hall, and by the sound of it they were giving out to her grandfather.

'Sophie! Come down here and meet your two grandaunts,' Grandfather called.

Sophie flushed. How did he know she was standing up above, listening? As she descended, she ran her fingers through her hair and made sure her cardigan was buttoned. Two sets of eyes watched every step she took until she reached the hall.

'Sophie! This is your Aunt Maud and your Aunt Dolores. They are my two sisters.'

Sophie gave a kind of curtsey.

The larger of the old women came forward and hugged her clumsily. She smelt of powder and lavender water. She looked like a big black crow with a black suit and a black silk hat, and a big black handbag.

'Welcome to Ireland, Sophie,' she said gruffly. 'London is

no place for children at the moment,' she added, staring intently at her grandniece.

'I'm your Aunt Dolores, child, but most people call me Dolly,' offered the other aunt, shaking Sophie by the hand kindly. 'I think you look rather like your mother, but I suspect you have the Fitzpatrick chin, just like Maud and your grandfather.'

'She's a bit pasty-looking!' said Aunt Maud.

'The sea air and good food will take care of that!' replied grandfather.

'Do they have nits?' questioned the black crow. 'Have you checked for that?'

'No, we do not have nits,' snapped Sophie.

'I heard a lot of the evacuees were covered in lice and nits,' Aunt Maud went on.

'If they had been, Maud, I think I am well capable of taking care of that problem,' said Grandfather firmly. 'I suppose we had better have tea,' he muttered, leading them towards the drawing room. 'Sophie, run down to the kitchen and ask Nancy to organise it!'

The housekeeper laughed when Sophie told her who the visitors were. 'Those two windbags always get your grandfather upset when they come. They'll be shouting and calling each other names before you know it! Run up and rescue him, Sophie!'

The three of them were sitting stiffly in their armchairs when Sophie pushed open the door. Grandfather was tapping his fingers on the padded armrest of his chair, something he always did when he was impatient.

Aunt Maud was busy filling her brother in with the local gossip, while Aunt Dolly was humming ever so slightly to herself.

Sophie smiled. Aunt Dolly looked nice. She had taken off her coat to reveal a pale mauve blouse and two necklaces of enormous beads which she played with as she pretended to listen to the others.

'Do you play an instrument?' she asked Sophie, nodding over towards the piano in the corner.

'No,' said Sophie, shaking her head regretfully.

'Pity!' said her aunt. 'Music is such a gift.'

Sophie hesitated. 'But I sing ... I mean, I like singing.'

The other two were listening now too.

'What kind of singing?' asked her aunt.

'Oh anything – folk, popular, hymns. In London I was in the church choir, and the school choir too.' Sophie blushed. It sounded like she was boasting.

'I hope to have the opportunity of hearing you sing some day. Perhaps you will come over to our house – and I will play the piano for you,' said Aunt Dolly.

Sophie smiled. 'That would be nice! Thank you.'

They were interrupted by the noisy arrival of Hugh. His hands and face were muddy and Sophie was conscious of how worn his clothes looked.

'I've been searching for a hedgehog,' he announced. 'I think we've got one in the garden.'

'So this is the boy?' Aunt Maud said.

Hugh stopped still, shifting awkwardly from one foot to the other.

Both women nodded at each other.

'Hugh, go wash your hands!' ordered Sophie crossly.

He was about to argue with her, but Grandfather nodded in the direction of the hall, so he cleared off.

'Ragamuffin!' murmured Aunt Dolly. 'The poor little mite!'

'Something has got to be done!' announced Aunt Maud, draining the last sip of her tea and replacing the delicate cup on the small polished tea table. Sophie knew that the 'something' included her.

Sophie thought it was strange that neither of the aunts mentioned Mum and Dad, or even enquired about them.

An hour later the two aunts began to gather their bags and daintily sweep the cake crumbs off their skirts.

'Sophie, you will come to visit me, won't you?' Aunt Dolly reminded her. Her face was small and pale and kind, with gentle green eyes that peeped out from ginger eyelashes.

'Now, Jerome, you won't forget what I told you. You know, Wicklow is a small place, and people do talk!' chided Aunt Maud. 'You will get those children fixed up, or would you prefer the two of us to sort it out?'

It was obvious that Grandfather was happy to leave the sorting out to his sisters, as the very next morning the two of them arrived to take the children to the local draper's shop.

Sophie reeled off quickly the brief list of clothes which

Hugh and she possessed. Both aunts shook their heads and tut-tutted.

Don't you know there's a war on? Sophie felt like shouting at them.

The shopkeeper welcomed the women who were obviously good customers. Given that it was wartime, Sophie was amazed how well stocked the shop was. In London there would have been queues outside it.

Hugh hated clothes-shopping, and was already getting edgy and gazing longingly out at the sun floating in through the open door, where a boy about his own age was crouched playing marbles on the tiled floor.

'Hugh, dear! Do pay attention!' pleaded Aunt Dolly. She had four or five jumpers dangling from her hand. 'Be a good boy and run and try these on.'

Hugh reluctantly took off his jumper and let the old lady slip the soft wool v-neck over his head. Sophie thought it was a bit pale, but the aunts liked it and kind of clapped and made Hugh walk around a bit and muttered to each other about the merits of pure wool and a good well-knitted rib. In the space of about half-an-hour they had got several shirts, three jumpers and short pants for him and five pairs of socks.

Hugh wanted long trousers but both aunts shook their heads in agreement: 'He's too young yet.' Hugh kicked at the corner of the glass display case in annoyance, but luckily they didn't notice.

The aunts also treated him to a pair of swimming trunks and light beach shoes and then, satisfied with Hugh's wardrobe, they turned their attention to Sophie.

Sophie was so embarrassed. She stood in front of the rail of 'little girl' dresses – the first three she had to try on were just awful. One was too short and pinched the top of her arms, one would simply not fasten and the third made her look like an overgrown doll. She didn't want to be rude but there was no way she was going to wear any of that stuff.

The drapery assistant was chatting away to the aunts while Sophie stood in the changing cubicle feeling miserable.

'Girls that age! That age is an awkward age, we always found it so. Perhaps something from the adult range?' Sophie could feel herself red-faced and hot and sweaty as a skirt like those her mother wore was handed in through the curtains to her.

'Too big!' she called to Aunt Maud.

Between the two of them the aunts searched every corner of the shop, leaving no rack or rail untouched in their quest to find something to suit.

Other customers came and went, buying underwear, a raincoat, summer shirts, and all seemed to stare in at Sophie, peeping out of the cubicle in her grubby, skinny vest.

At last there was nothing suitable left to try and Sophie gratefully grabbed her own dress and cardigan and dragged them back on.

Hugh's pile of clothes was huge while hers was small – some underwear, a new nightgown, a few pairs of socks, a lavender-coloured cardigan, a plain white shirt with a pocket and a horrible floral-patterned skirt.

The aunts seemed pleased with themselves.

Sophie watched as the shopkeeper began to wrap the parcels.

'By any chance,' she asked the assistant shyly, 'would you have a swimming suit for me?'

The woman opened a drawer in the cabinet behind her.

'Any of these should fit. Which would you like?' she asked, spreading them out on the glass counter.

Sophie fingered them and eventually settled on a ruched pale-blue suit with a narrow bodice and straps that tied around the neck, and a very slight skirt with a pattern of shells and little fish in white and orange on it.

'What were we thinking of, Maud? Imagine forgetting a swimsuit and us all living in Greystones!' exclaimed Aunt Dolly.

'Well, I think we've finished now!' replied Aunt Maud. 'What do you think, Dolly?'

'Oh yes, most definitely,' her sister agreed.

'On the account!' They both said in unison. The assistant headed for a red-covered book. 'Jerome's account, that is,' continued Aunt Maud. 'I mean Professor Fitzpatrick. He's their grandfather, you know.'

'Now, we must have tea,' she announced as they left the shop, and they headed for the magnificent hotel on the seafront.

Sophie had been curious about it. Every time she passed by she would look longingly through the gate or over the hedge that surrounded the perfect green lawn. Passing by you would hear the chatter and laughter of guests drift across to the road.

The four of them walked into the wide hallway and the children followed their aunts to a large comfortable drawing room with french doors looking out on the sweep of lawn, edged with a multicoloured border of flowers.

Hugh was hopping up and down with excitement, but Sophie tried to act nonchalant, as if she was used to visiting such places.

Aunt Maud ordered a pot of tea and cakes, and for Sophie and Hugh a jug of lemonade.

Sophie sat down on a big plush chair. What in heaven's name would she talk to these two women about?

CHAPTER 18

The Keepsake

Aunt Maud and Aunt Dolly sipped their milky tea slowly, while the children gulped down glasses of the freshly-made lemonade. Shopping definitely made you thirsty! Hugh eyed the cake-stand greedily and put a chocolate slice on his plate.

Two or three elderly couples came over to say hello to the aunts, and they chatted about the weather and golf and a game of bridge. They seemed curious about the two strange children. 'Jerome's grandchildren!' was the only answer they were given. The children smiled politely. Sophie could see a flicker of surprise in the old people's eyes at this information.

The grandaunts were a totally different kettle of fish when they were away from Grandfather, and they quizzed Sophie in detail about their lives in London. Where did they live? What size was their house? Did they have any help in the house? What school was she going to? Did they have to pay fees?

Hugh gave Sophie an elbow in the ribs and became unusually silent.

Sophie wanted to be friendly to the two old ladies but not indiscreet, and there was the question of loyalty to Mum and Dad. She did her best to seem jolly and friendly, but after an hour of it her head ached, trying to remember what to say and what not to say.

Two spots of red flared in Aunt Maud's gaunt cheeks when Sophie told her about Mum and the hospital. 'What's her condition, Sophie? What's the prognosis?' She was all attention as Sophie outlined her mother's illness and what the nurse had told her.

'The very best of nursing! That's what the children's mother needs. Mark my words, Dolly!' Aunt Maud stated.

'Well, I'm sure that all concerned are doing their very best,' said Aunt Dolly, patting Sophie's hand. 'You know, child, how sorry we are about Libby, we're keeping her in our prayers.'

Finally, the aunts called the waiter and settled the bill.

'I know, Sophie, we didn't get much for you today,' said Aunt Dolly.

'Perhaps a trip on the train to Dublin?' murmured Aunt Maud, rummaging in her handbag, 'nice shops there, almost as good as London, fine style for a girl your age. We'll mention it to Jerome.'

'Thank you,' said Sophie politely, secretly aghast at the thought of another shopping trip.

'I feel sick!' whispered Hugh.

Any wonder, thought Sophie – he'd been stuffing himself for the last hour.

'If you don't mind,' she said, 'I think I'd better take Hugh home, he's not feeling very well.'

'We'll walk with you,' offered the grandaunts.

'No, honestly, it's better we go on our own, we're nearly home already. Thank you so much for all you've done.'

Sophie kissed the two sets of powdered cheeks politely. She grabbed Hugh and the parcels, and the two of them chased back to the relative peace and quiet of Carrigraun.

Early next morning Hugh dressed himself in his new clothes. Sophie smiled to herself. He definitely looked healthier than he had done before they came to Ireland. His shoulders seemed to have broadened a bit, and his skinny legs didn't seem quite as bandy. His face was losing that scared, pinched, tense look, which, now that she thought about it, many of the kids back home had.

She pulled him close. 'You know I love you, Hugh!'

'Course you do! You're my big sister,' he smiled shyly.

'And you're the best brother anyone could have!' She felt so lucky to have him. She fixed the shoulder of his new jumper. 'And you look very handsome!' she said.

Hugh smirked. Nobody had ever told him that before. 'Well, I think you're getting prettier too,' he complimented her in return.

Sophie laughed, even if it wasn't true. She hadn't changed, she was still plain old Sophie. Her hair was maybe a bit shinier from the soft water, and the sea breeze had already turned her normally white skin to a soft golden colour, but it would take more than a week by the sea to make her any bit pretty.

'Come on, Hugh! We'd better hurry or we'll be late for breakfast!'

Grandfather was engrossed in his newspaper, and barely

nodded at them. Nancy had told them he used to get all the newspapers but now because of paper shortages he was trying to restrict himself to one, which he read from front to back.

Hugh stood in front of him and coughed. Grandfather looked up.

'Well, Hugh, my boy! They say clothes maketh the man. I'm not sure about that, but there is most definitely an improvement.' Hugh's eyes sparkled with the compliment. 'Good to have got rid of all those old clothes of yours, I bet!' he added absentmindedly, turning over a page.

Sophie stopped eating. 'Grandfather!' The old man kept on reading. She made a swipe at the page, disturbing him. 'What did you do with Hugh's old clothes?' she asked earnestly.

'Eat your breakfast, girl! Don't be letting good food get cold!'

'The clothes!' she demanded angrily.

'Sophie! What on earth are you on about? I told Nancy to get rid of Hugh's old clothes.'

Sophie jumped up from the chair and raced out to the kitchen, where the housekeeper was making a fresh pot of tea.

'Nancy! What did you do with Hugh's old clothes?' she demanded.

'Oh, I put them out in the bin. Why?'

Sophie ran across the red tiles and out the back door to the yard. There were two bins standing against the fence. One was very smelly, obviously full of food scraps. She lifted the lid off the other one. Immediately, she spotted the familiar piece of grey hand-knitting and dragged it out, clutching it to her.

'Oh! Oh!' she sighed with relief.

Nancy stood in the doorway watching her. 'Sophie, are you all right? You know I wouldn't do anything to offend you!'

Sophie nodded, not trusting herself to speak. She walked back to the dining room.

'Do you see this?' she said, brandishing the outgrown grey jumper. 'My mother knitted this for my little brother. She managed to get the wool somehow or other, and she sat by the fire, night after night, knitting it. She put in that blue stripe, to match his eyes.'

'Calm down, girl!' remonstrated Grandfather, laying down the newspaper.

'With the rest of the wool,' continued Sophie, 'she made a pair of socks for Dad so his army issue boots wouldn't hurt so bad. Mum hates knitting – she's always dropping stitches and forgetting to count rows. It makes her eyes water, and gets her cross.' She shook the ragged-looking jumper under Grandfather's nose. 'But still she knitted this ... remember, Hugh ... and Mum nearly died trying to get this jumper ... she went out to the washing ...'

It was no use. Two pairs of bewildered male eyes focused on her.

'You! You don't understand a thing!' she screamed at her grandfather. 'You have your big house, your furniture, your pictures, your ornaments, your precious books, while we've got nothing – no house, not a room, nothing left that is just ours.' Sophie clasped the jumper to her. 'I'm keeping it!' she said firmly. She took it upstairs and hid it under her pillow.

Back downstairs, Grandfather was waiting for her. Hugh had made himself scarce.

'I apologise, Sophie!' Grandfather told her. 'It was thoughtless of me. It was all my fault, not Nancy's. I should have consulted you and Hugh about your things.' She nodded silently. 'You miss London, and naturally you miss your parents and friends. Greystones and I are a poor substitute for home and hearth.' She could tell by the way he was rubbing his beard that he was trying to figure out what to say to her next. 'I did tell your Aunt Jessica my reservations about evacuating you to Ireland and my taking the two of you,' he continued.

'We are grateful, honestly, Grandfather,' she interrupted.

'One has to do one's duty, what is expected. It's the least I could do in the circumstances,' he added.

Duty. Like a cold grey stone off the beach, the word pressed down on Sophie, making her feel breathless. Duty – that's all she and Hugh were to this stranger, whom they called Grandfather. She stared at him, but he had already retrieved his newspaper.

'Excuse me, Grandfather!' she whispered politely, 'I think I'll go and find Hugh.' He didn't even look up, as with tears welling in her eyes she ran from the room.

CHAPTER 19

Blue Skies

The seagulls screeched and whirled above them in the bright blue sky as spring drifted lazily towards summer and the days got longer. Grandfather wanted the two of them to start in the local schools.

'It's hardly worth it!' Sophie protested. 'It's only a few weeks to the summer holidays and we'll be back in England by the autumn.'

'That makes no difference,' argued Grandfather. 'I'm not having the two of you miss out on your education just because you're here in Ireland. Learning is the very cornerstone of society. You must go to school!'

Sophie sensed his determination, and gave in.

The convent school wasn't bad. The nuns were as kind as they could be to the little English evacuee who had been landed on them. Hugh attended the boys' primary school, and Sophie couldn't believe how well he settled in and made friends. She envied her younger brother as he raced around the yard with Donal and Liam, two of the boys in his class, looking as if he hadn't a care in the world.

She hated to admit it, but she was the one finding it hard to get used to the change. Sister Agnes, her teacher, did her best to integrate Sophie with the other girls and to encourage her to make new friends. But Sophie felt very much and outsider and she kept mostly to herself.

She noticed that the others all talked about 'the emergency' but to her, coming from the London Blitz, it was most definitely 'the war'.

The school work was easy enough, and she couldn't resist putting her hand up to answer the nun's questions, ignoring the giggles from the back row and the girls who mimicked her London accent. They had already nicknamed her Miss Clever-clogs.

As soon as school was over she and Hugh wasted no time in getting to the beach and harbour, where the fresh sea air left them dizzy and full of a strange new kind of energy.

They both loved the harbour and spent hours playing on the shingle among the boats. There were all kinds of boats there lying in the sun, some sanded and varnished and tended with love and care, others scarred with years of neglect, with peeling paint and leaky bottoms where pools of dirty water stagnated.

The war seemed a very long way off, except for the awful loneliness of missing Mum and Dad, and wishing that they were a family again.

Every evening before tea, Grandfather would walk from one end of the long winding seafront to the other. Sophie often watched him in the distance. He walked as briskly as his bad leg would allow, sometimes stopping to nod politely to those he met along the way. He had a set routine and disliked having it disturbed.

Back at the house, Nancy was set on feeding the two of

them up, making them drink big glasses of creamy Jersey milk from Wicklow cows and cooking the best meals ever from whatever foods were in good supply – beef and lamb, eggs and fish and bacon, and fresh vegetables straight from the garden.

Grandfather had taken to letting the children listen to the wireless in the late evenings. He moved the set from his study into the drawing room, dusting it off and placing it on a mahogany sideboard. There was a special programme for children who had been evacuated and were far from home – in Wales, Scotland, Canada and the USA mostly – and Sophie and Hugh loved to join in all the songs. Grandfather stayed while these programmes were on, watching silently. Perhaps he thought they were silly with their marching songs and their funny verses. Sophie didn't really care. The programme was a link with children just like her all over the world, and their home called out to them over the air waves:

> *Goodnight children, everywhere ...*
> *And though you're far away*
> *You'll go home one day.*
> *Goodnight children, everywhere.*

CHAPTER 20

Dark Waters

One Saturday morning, Sophie sat on the wall, watching the curve of the harbour and its protective arm formed by the mountains and Bray Head, while down below on the beach Hugh and his friend Donal messed around in the boats.

She had stayed up late the night before, writing letters to Mum and Dad and Aunt Jessie. She had them in her pocket ready to post.

'Hugh!' she shouted, trying to get his attention. 'I have to go to the post office. Come on! We'll be back in a few minutes!'

He was engrossed playing pirates with his friend and he was deliberately ignoring her.

'Hugh!'

'I don't want to go!' he shouted at her.

'*Hugh!*'

'You go! I'll stay here with Donal,' he promised.

'Oh, all right then!' she agreed reluctantly. 'I won't be long.'

Sophie jumped off the wall, leaving the boys to their game. She walked up past the hotel entrance to Mrs Murphy's shop. The shopkeeper, with her blond curly-haired baby resting on her hip, waved to Sophie. Sophie waved back, then ran on past the church and finally entered the stuffy stillness of the post office.

There was a queue ahead of her and she tapped her foot impatiently, making the man in front glare at her.

Her three letters were ready to go across the sea, all full of good news and cheerful things – things that sometimes gave her a feeling of such tightness in her throat and chest while she wrote them that she often had to put her pen down. Her Mum must never know about the nights she lay still in her bed with hot tears scalding her eyes and cheeks. Aunt Jessie must never know how she longed for someone to laugh and chat with so she would not feel so alone, and Dad must never realise that her sleep was haunted by bad dreams of bombs and bullets and of him being wounded or dead.

She posted the letters and ran back towards the harbour. A small crowd had gathered on the North Beach. Sophie wondered what they were doing. Was Hugh there in the middle of it all? In an instant she spotted Donal, his young face white and scared – and why had Mr Kinsella, his father, waded out into the water up to his chest? Two other fishermen were shouting and pointing at something.

Where was Hugh? She scanned the crowd carefully, searching for him.

A woman who had been sitting reading came up beside Sophie. 'Apparently it's some poor child,' she said, 'fell off a boat. The whole thing nearly capsized!'

Warning bells sounded in Sophie's head. She could hear the gushing sound of water in her ears as she began to race, tumbling and tripping over the large uneven stones.

'It wasn't my fault, Sophie!' pleaded Donal. 'We were taking turns pushing each other in and out and holding the rope. I dropped the rope and Hugh got scared. I told him to sit down and stay still and I'd get him, but he was trying to climb out or something and the boat went over to one side and he slipped in.'

'Oh my God! Where is he?' Sophie rushed headlong into the water. Mr Kinsella was lifting something up – it was her brother. His head flopped against the fisherman's chest and his arms and legs dangled limply. His eyes were closed and his lips and face were almost totally blue.

The fisherman brushed Sophie aside and carried Hugh up onto the beach where he laid him on a coat that someone had spread out on the ground. He tilted Hugh's head back and put his large hand across the boy's pale neck.

'Come on, lad. You're safe. We got you out. Come on, lad.'

Sophie crouched on the stones beside him. 'Hugh, don't do this. Do you hear me? Don't do this!' She pulled at the cold wet hand and arm.

Hugh's eyelashes seemed to move, something was stirring within him. A bubbling, choking kind of cough came from his throat.

'Over you go, lad!' Mr Kinsella rolled him gently to one side.

Water burst out of Hugh's mouth and from the pinched whiteness of his nostrils, and he splurted and gagged.

A huge sigh of relief swelled from the crowd of people around.

'The boy's all right!'

'Gave us a right scare but he's safe now!'

'Nearly drowned, you know!'

Mr Kinsella and Sophie knelt down beside Hugh. They were both soaking wet too and already Sophie was beginning to feel cold despite the sun.

'I'm sorry, Soph!' Hugh began to cry a funny kind of cry, as if he couldn't get his breath.

'Don't talk, Hugh lad! Save your breath!' advised Mr Kinsella.

Hugh's teeth started to chatter and he began to shiver, his lips moving as if he were praying.

A woman interrupted them. 'The boy's in shock. We'd better get him home and get a doctor for him!'

Sophie snapped out of the slow weary feeling that clung to her. 'We live up at the seafront and my grandfather – we live with him – is a doctor,' she offered.

'They're the Fitzpatrick children, y'know,' someone said.

The woman nodded. 'Very well! My car is parked across the road. I'll drive you all home.'

The fisherman lifted Hugh up and laid him gently on a rug in the back of the old grey Austin. Sophie sat beside him. The woman gestured to Mr Kinsella to get in the front.

'I'm all wet, Ma'am. Maybe it would be better if I just walked home,' he protested.

But she wouldn't hear of it. 'You're all soaked through. You'll end up with pneumonia if you don't get warm and dry straight away. It's the very least I can do.'

Seconds later they were outside the door of Carrigraun. Sophie could see the surprise on Nancy's face when she opened the front door to the wet, bedraggled party. Grandfather was called.

'What in heaven's name is it, woman?' he shouted at Nancy as he came down into the hall, limping badly. His grey hair was muzzy and he looked tired. He'd been having a nap.

Nancy led him upstairs to Hugh's bedroom. She undressed the boy quickly and dried him with a huge warm towel, before putting a fresh pair of pyjamas on him and pulling the blankets over him. Hugh lay exhausted, small and pale against the bulky white starched pillowcase.

Grandfather sent Sophie down to his study to fetch his black leather doctor's bag.

First, Grandfather put on the old-fashioned stethoscope and lifted Hugh's pyjama top to listen to his heart. All the time he talked in a reassuring hushed tone. The others waited on the landing as the doctor completed the examination.

His face was serious when he came out to them. 'Hugh will be fine. He's had a very bad shock and is naturally freezing cold. I'll keep a good eye on that chest, but with any luck he should be fine.'

'Oh that's wonderful news!' sighed the woman who had driven them home.

Grandfather shook Donal's father by the hand once they got downstairs. 'Thank you so much, Mr Kinsella. I ... my family are forever in your debt. My son Neil would be ...' he paused, finding it difficult to go on '... very very grateful.'

Sophie stared – he had actually mentioned her father, said his name.

Donal's father was beginning to get cold. He pulled the rug around his shoulders as he got back into the front seat of the car.

'Thank you!' they all called, as they waved a subdued goodbye.

'Come on, Sophie. I'll run a bath for you,' offered Nancy, 'then into bed with you for a while.'

Grandfather was back inside, talking to Hugh. Shaken and exhausted, Sophie was glad to relax in the steamy hot bath. Nancy had left out some fresh clothes for her and Sophie pulled them on, beginning to feel relief ease through her veins. She peeped in on Hugh – he was fast asleep and though he still looked pale, he had curled himself into his usual shape and looked more normal. Back in her bedroom, Sophie stared out the window, watching people passing up and down the seafront. It was hard to believe that only an hour ago she nearly lost Hugh. It was my fault, she told herself. I should have minded him. He's my responsibility. Why did I leave him? She reproached herself a hundred times over, feeling guiltier and guiltier by the minute.

But it was nothing to how she felt after her grandfather had words with her.

They were sitting at the table, both silent, waiting for Nancy to serve the tea – she had already taken some warm milk and fingers of toast up to Hugh.

Grandfather was seething with rage and anger which seemed to be totally directed at Sophie.

'Well, what do you have to say for yourself?' he demanded.

She said nothing, just sat staring at the fine bone china cup.

'I hope you learnt your lesson today!' he continued.

Sophie nodded. 'I'm sorry, Grandfather. Truly sorry.'

'Sorry! *Sorry!*' he shouted. 'Well, that's just not good enough. Your brother almost drowns and that's all you can say. Sorry! Like some stupid little ninny!'

'I didn't mean for it to happen, Grandfather,' pleaded Sophie. 'I only left him for a few minutes while I went up the road to the post office with some letters. I was no time at all.'

'You were gone long enough for your young brother to almost drown himself.'

'I know,' she added softly.

'If I can't trust you it means I'll have to forbid the two of you from going down to the harbour or beach. I am responsible to your parents and to the authorities for you. Obviously neither of you has an ounce of sense,' he shouted angrily. 'Why in heaven's name didn't Neil teach you to swim?'

Sophie took a deep breath. 'Grandfather, you have never even cared to ask, but Hugh and I live in an ordinary house in London, we have only ever been to the seaside two or three times in our lives on day trips – that's as much as Mum and Dad could manage. I know it's my fault totally what happened so please don't try and blame my Dad,' she sobbed.

'You are a stupid, self-centred girl who was too busy daydreaming to take proper care of your brother!' said the old man, his eyes hard and cold.

'I hate you!' shouted Sophie, jumping to her feet. 'My Dad hates you and now I do too. You're the horriblest grandfather anyone could ever have.' She was screaming now.

Sophie felt the stinging slap of his palm across her face. She almost stopped breathing with the shock of it. She turned and fled from the drawing room out through the hallway towards the front door.

She ran down the driveway, across the road and found herself making for the rocks. She scrambled lightly over them, using her hands to steady herself where it was slippery, until she reached a good vantage point. Down below, the sea swirled menacingly. She closed her eyes, thinking of Hugh underneath the water, fighting for air and breath. It was hard to believe that this sparkling blue friend that soothed and calmed her could in turn be so dangerous. She stared at the water, watching the rhythmic swell of foaming bubbles below.

Sophie sat for a long time as the rocks beneath her cooled and the sea became darker, and slurped and slapped against the jagged rock which reached out like a finger from the shore. Soon the moon would come out – the sun had already disappeared, hiding behind the Sugarloaf mountains. In the fading light between night and day she sent a secret message, willing it to reach a soldier far away and a woman lying in a hospital bed. 'Stay well! Stay safe! Your children need you! I need you! I need you so much!'

She was beginning to feel cold and her leg was stiff, so she had to stand up and stretch. Hugh might have woken up and he might want her. She kept her eyes down as she walked up the driveway, ignoring the tall stern figure staring out at her from the bay window.

CHAPTER 21

Wartimes

Hugh had a few days off school after the accident, and Sophie walked the few minutes there and back on her own. In a small corner, deep inside her, she hid her loneliness and fear.

Grandfather and Sophie barely spoke to each other nowadays. They were polite for appearances' sake, but a clear battleline of dislike divided them firmly.

Nancy shook her head in bewilderment. 'For a slip of a thing, you're a right stubborn lassie, Sophie! Make it up with him! He is your grandfather, after all, he deserves some respect!' But Sophie would stick her head in whatever library book she was reading and ignore the unwanted advice.

Hugh was puzzled about it all but he knew that Grandfather still blamed Sophie for what had happened. The old man refused to listen to Hugh's explanations, saying that he was too young to understand responsibility.

Aunt Jessie had written back to Sophie. Her letter was the only thing that had made Sophie smile for a long time. She was helping with the lambs and the calves and she sent a photo of herself standing like a farmer's wife in amongst the livestock. She had visited Mum and said the doctors were very pleased with her progress. She also mentioned that Dad might be due some home-leave soon. How Sophie longed to see them all again.

Grandfather insisted that they were to have swimming lessons now that the sea was getting warmer. Each day they went down to the small dock area, once the tide was in, where a very jolly woman called Virginia gave them lessons. Up to now Sophie had only splashed and waded in the water, or jumped up and down in it. But she loved the way her body floated in the salty water, her arms and legs feeling so light, as Virginia looked on.

'Sophie! I think you might be part mermaid!' joked Virginia.

Sophie laughed, but secretly felt it too. The sea was her friend and learning to swim was giving her such happiness, she couldn't believe it.

Hugh found it harder. He would dog-paddle frantically, grabbing at Sophie in a panic. Virginia or Sophie would keep a hand under Hugh's tummy, helping him to stay up in the water, or hold his chin so he wouldn't swallow big gulps of water.

'You must relax and keep calm in the water!' the teacher told him over and over again.

Hugh was determined to learn. Grandfather had forbidden him to put a foot in a boat again until he could swim.

The war was getting worse. The Germans had bombed Coventry, destroying factories where British planes were made. Now Greece and Yugoslavia were being taken over by the German Army. Bit by bit, it seemed, every part of Europe was becoming involved in the war, the fighting spilling from one country to the next. Ireland was only across the sea from England – what would happen if Hitler and the Germans decided to take Ireland, to use it as a base to attack England?

'How long will it go on, Grandfather?' asked Hugh.

'Who can say, child, but from the way things are going, probably a whole lot longer than any of us ever imagined.'

'Oh!' said Hugh. Sophie was unsure if her brother was disappointed or not.

America was helping Mr Churchill to get food and supplies to England, and Grandfather reckoned it wouldn't be too long before Russia would become embroiled too.

The announcer's voice was unusually sombre one evening as he announced that London had been bombed very badly the night before and that thousands had died. Please God let Mummy be safe, prayed Sophie, silently, relieved to be far away from the city. The British had bombed Berlin, so now the Germans had bombed London again. It was a tit-for-tat war they were playing, and Sophie couldn't understand it.

'In Belfast ...' the announcer continued.

Sophie gasped. '*Belfast!*'

Grandfather put down his pen to listen.

'... for seven hours, the important harbour and docks area has been bombarded.'

They listened to the report of the huge damage inflicted by the Luftwaffe. Hundreds had been killed, thousands left homeless. Belfast – the city that built the ships for Britain in its mighty shipyards – was totally stunned. Belfast was ablaze.

Mr De Valera, the Irish prime minister, ordered ambulances and firemen and firebrigades from the south of Ireland to go to help.

A shiver ran through Sophie as she thought of London destroyed and now Belfast. The war was getting nearer. She didn't want to feel scared again.

CHAPTER 22

All Hands Lost!

One afternoon Sophie came home from school to find Nancy crying. Dirty delph and dishes lay piled in the sink. Something was burning in the stove. Nancy was sitting hunched up in the middle of it all.

Sophie stood at the kitchen door, unsure of what to do or say. 'What ever's the matter, Nancy?' she asked.

Nancy began to sob louder than ever, a huge gulping kind of crying that seemed to go through every bone in her body.

'Nancy, please! What's wrong?'

The housekeeper looked up – it was as if she hardly saw Sophie standing there. 'All hands lost! That's what the telegram said,' she intoned in a strange, dead kind of voice. 'No hope of survivors.'

Sophie gasped. It must be her brother Frank. He was in the British Merchant Navy.

'Frank attacked by a U-boat, blown to bits in the ocean – food for the fishes!' Nancy wailed.

'Don't say that, Nancy!' pleaded Sophie, grasping her by the hands, 'he could still be alive, floating in the water. A friend of my father's survived after a mine blew his boat up. He floated in the sea for two days with his lifebelt till they found him.'

'He's gone! I can sense it. Me and Frank – you know there's

only a year and a bit between us. People used to call us the twins when we were small.' Sophie could understand that. Nancy had shown her a photo of a smiling red-haired young man, and they were the image of each other.

'And like twins we always had a sense about each other. He's left this life. I can tell it. I have this empty feeling here in the middle of my stomach.' Nancy began to wail again.

The kitchen door opened and Hugh peered in. 'What's for tea?' he asked.

Sophie glared at him.

Then Grandfather appeared. He looked weary as he came over to Nancy. 'I'm sorry, my dear, so sorry about Frank. He was a good sort of fellah. Those north Atlantic waters are treacherous.'

'Oh, Professor! What about my Mam and Dad? It'll kill them!'

'Sophie, put on the kettle for a cup of tea!' he ordered, 'and turn off that blasted pot of whatever is cooking.'

'I'm sorry. I just totally forgot about the tea,' apologised the red-eyed young woman.

'Listen, Nancy, I phoned Dolly, and she and Maud are coming over. They'll drive you back to Ashford,' Grandfather told her gently. 'Plenty of sugar in that tea, Sophie!' he added.

Sophie and Hugh were then sent to the front room to keep watch for the car turning into the driveway.

They left their grandfather holding Nancy's hand and talking in a way Sophie would not have believed possible. He seemed so kind and caring. Compassionate. Yes, that was the word. It was a side of him that she had never seen before.

The car pulled into the driveway with Aunt Dolly driving. The children ran to tell Grandfather they had arrived. They watched as the adults helped the normally boisterous Nancy into the car as if she were an invalid.

'It's a time to be with your family, Nancy,' said Grandfather. 'So take as long as you need and don't be worrying about us. We'll manage.'

Sophie eyed him – why did he have to say that? She wished Nancy didn't have to go. Then she felt selfish and guilty.

He nodded in her direction. 'Young Sophie and I will keep things running ship-shape.'

Ship-shape indeed! thought Sophie. That probably meant him giving orders and herself and Hugh following them.

When the old car had set off along the seafront Grandfather banged the front door shut. 'Young fellows dying for no good reason – that's what this damned war is all about ...' They did not hear the rest as he slammed his study door in anger.

That night they had sandwiches, big chunky doorstep ones and mugs of milky cocoa, on their own in the kitchen. It made Sophie think of home, of London, of the shelters and of the awful sadness of war.

CHAPTER 23

Porridge and Curry

Porridge for breakfast. That's what they were to have every morning in Nancy's absence. None of this messing around trying to fry things.

'A big bowl of porridge to set you up for the day!' That's what Grandfather said.

Hugh hated it. He played with it, tracing the letter H on its thick gluey surface.

'Makes you grow! Builds muscles!' advised Grandfather.

But still Hugh would barely pick at it.

Grandfather doused his in salt from the silver salt cellar on the table. As a concession he let Sophie fetch the honey pot, shaped like a yellow beehive, with one quaint-looking pottery bee on it, and spoon a circle of runny gold onto the steaming porridge. At least that made it a little better.

The house seemed quiet and gloomy without Nancy. Sophie did her best to keep out of Grandfather's way. He was in a strange humour – more lively, but often more grumpy too.

A woman who worked for Aunt Dolly came to help with the laundry two days a week, but the rest of the time they had to manage by themselves.

One afternoon the kitchen was full of strange smells and Sophie found Grandfather chopping up all kinds of things and putting them in a big pot on the stove – meat, vegetables, apples, some nuts, spices.

'Can I help, Grandfather?' she volunteered warily.

'Not now,' he said. 'But there will be plates and dishes to wash afterwards.' Whatever was in the pot, it took ages to cook, and Sophie and Hugh were starving by the time he brought it to the table.

'What is it?' enquired Hugh, suspicious.

It smelt strong.

'Just try it,' chided Grandfather. 'I used to have this many years ago. Here's some chutney to mix in with it.'

Sophie thought it looked good. Hugh watched her as she put a forkful in her mouth. The taste was different – then within two seconds it seemed like her mouth was on fire! Even her eyes started to water. She wanted to spit it out but instead she forced herself to swallow it. Then she jumped up and ran to the kitchen for a glass of water to cool her mouth. She brought a large jugful back to the table with her.

Grandfather was amused, but she noticed that he too filled his glass to the brim and gulped it down. 'Perhaps I was rather heavy-handed with the curry spices,' he reflected.

Curry! That's what it was! Sophie remembered her Mum teasing her dad if he made any negative comments about her cooking; she'd ask: 'Well, will I make you a curry, then?' Grandfather obviously used to make them when he was younger.

Sophie tried it again. It didn't seem as hot this time, and the spicy taste – well, there was something that made you want to eat it; in fact, after a few tentative forkfuls, she actually began to enjoy it! Hugh ate the rice and picked at the bits of lamb, but it was clear that he didn't like it.

'Eat up!' Grandfather ordered.

Hugh ignored him.

'Didn't you hear me, boy? Children are going hungry all over Europe and you leave a plate of good food in front of you.'

'I don't want it, Grandfather, I won't eat it! It's disgusting!' Hugh said with feeling, shoving the plate at the old man.

Grandfather glared at him. 'I will not have good food wasted!'

'Why can't we have nice food, nice teas like my mummy used to make?' Hugh demanded. Sophie detected a wobble in her small brother's voice.

Grandfather softened. 'Young man, I know I'm a poor substitute for your mother, but I ... I'm doing my damned best!'

Sophie butted in. 'Listen, Hugh, there are two eggs in the pantry and I'll make some scrambled eggs in a few minutes.'

'Boys that age – you forget their taste buds haven't developed properly,' muttered the old man. 'Nursery food, that's all they're able for.'

Next day Aunt Dolly arrived with a steak-and-kidney pie which she reheated for them. Hugh ate an enormous portion, as if to make up for Grandfather's cooking.

'Jerome's such a fancy cook,' Aunt Dolly announced, as she ladled out the pie, 'when he *does* cook, that is! Have you had his famous Indian curry yet?'

The children giggled and Grandfather blushed.

'Now, don't go making that fancy stuff, Jerome,' chided Aunt Dolly. 'Good plain cooking is what's good for you.'

After that, Grandfather more or less stuck to meat and potatoes, but he complained about how boring it was. Sophie felt he was irritated again by their being there – he couldn't have things just the way he wanted them.

She discovered that Grandfather was very finicky about small things too. He constantly complained about the amount of sand the two children tracked through the house. 'Clean up that sand!' he'd bark at them, no matter how much they'd swept already.

But Sophie said nothing. After every meal she cleaned the dining room, insisting that Hugh help her clear off the table, and then she tackled the kitchen. Grandfather always left a terrible mess – used pots and pans were piled up, bits of gristle he'd cut off the meat were left lying about on the table, potato skins scattered on the chopping board, vegetable peelings in the sink. Yet he expected the kitchen, pantry and scullery to be gleaming when he'd inspect it later. It always took her ages to sort it out.

Then, she noticed some things beginning to go short in the pantry. They needed more sugar and tea, and another pot of honey for the morning porridge. She decided to make a list, but wondered should she give it to Grandfather? Would he be cross with her?

She propped the list up against the tea-caddy before going

to bed one night, hoping he'd notice it. In the morning there was a note in its place: *Provisions will be delivered by lunchtime. Jerome Fitzpatrick*

They were now truly like strangers, sending notes to each other, Sophie thought sadly.

CHAPTER 24

A Little on the Lonely Side

For two days Sophie and Grandfather avoided each other. Hugh was scared by the silence and enmity between these two people who were supposed to be minding him.

School was dull. The other children seemed to sense Sophie's need to be alone, and they left her to her own devices. Sister Agnes called her to her desk after class one day. Sophie thought at first she had made some mistake in her schoolwork.

'No, child!' said the kindly old nun. 'It's nothing like that, but I do worry about you. You sit there with a faraway look in your eyes!' Sophie blushed. 'I'm not criticising,' the teacher continued, 'it must be very difficult being so far from home, but now that you are here, do try and give the school and your classmates a chance. We all need to have friends,' she added, softly.

'I have friends, lots of them, but they're all evacuated too!' protested Sophie.

'You may be in Ireland for some time yet, Sophie. The war may go on for a long, long time. Why don't you try to make things a little easier for yourself?'

But Sophie just wanted to be on her own. She spent a lot of her time walking up and down the seafront, watching the waves and the tides, or sitting on the rocks, or on the edge of the pier with the sea as her companion.

Hugh ran wild with his crowd of boys, a small thin figure trying to keep up with the rest of them as they messed around with the boats on the beach. She knew she should spend more time with her little brother – talk to him, play with him. So, one afternoon she called him. 'Hugh! Will we go down to the beach to play?'

His eyes lit up, like a small dog being taken out for a long-overdue walk, and all along the way he never stopped talking.

They picked the biggest, best empty boat lying up on the beach and climbed in.

'We're going to a treasure island,' shouted Hugh, pretending to be the captain. Sophie was his crew and had to take orders as the boat was attacked by pirates, an octopus and a shark, one after another – all of which the brave captain fought off single-handed.

Sophie wasn't really in a pirate mood. She stared out across the water – on the far side was England, a country at war, while here in Ireland there was peace. Everything she loved and cared about was on the other side of that sea.

'Sophie! What are you doing?' interrupted Hugh peevishly.

'I'm just thinking, Hugh, remembering.'

'I find it hard to remember,' he said, and a look of sorrow clouded his small freckled face. 'Sometimes I think I'm going to forget Dad, the way he looks and talks.'

'No, you won't, Hugh!' said Sophie reassuringly.

'I remember the chips and sausages and the apple tart we

had for tea the night before he went away, but I can't remember what he said to me when I ran down to the gate after him,' Hugh sighed.

'He said you were the best boy, the best son a man could have,' said Sophie softly, 'and he told me to take care of you!'

'Or Mum's face, her hair, what her eyes are like! I'm forgetting her too,' he said anxiously.

'No! You're not, Hugh!' Sophie told him fiercely. 'I won't let you forget them, I promise!' This was what the war was doing, she thought, breaking up families, sending children away from the people they loved.

'Sometimes I try to dream that things are back the way they used to be, just all ordinary again,' he muttered, his face looking drawn and his bony knuckles white against the side of the boat.

'I like "ordinary" too,' sighed Sophie.

'I do like Greystones, but that doesn't mean I want to forget London,' Hugh said firmly.

'Of course not, silly!' she joked, ruffling his hair.

Some instinct made Sophie look up, and in the distance she saw Grandfather out for his usual seafront walk. He had stopped and was looking down at them. Sophie pretended not to see his tall bulky figure and ignored the wave of greeting he gave her.

Hugh raised his head, following her glance.

'Look, Soph! It's Grandfather!'

'Don't wave at him, Hugh!' she ordered crossly, 'he might come down to us.'

Hugh looked puzzled. He would never understand it. His big sister and his grandfather never seemed to be able to get along or even be nice to each other.

'I think Grandfather is lonely too!' suggested Hugh.

Sophie refused to answer. 'Come on, Captain Hugh!' she said, trying to distract him. 'The crew is ready to set sail again!'

Hugh put his worries aside, and plunged back into the world of make-believe.

CHAPTER 25

Torpedoed!

Sophie tossed and turned in bed that night. Then, in the darkness, she heard a voice. Within a few seconds she realised it was Hugh, talking in his sleep. Worried, she got out of her bed and went to his room.

Hugh lay with the blankets half kicked off, and he was thrashing about and turning in the bed. His hair was damp and clung to his head, and he was obviously deep in a vivid nightmare.

'Hugh! Hugh! It's all right! Wake up!' Sophie called softly.

But he seemed too far away, in a world where he could not hear her.

She could see a pulse throbbing in his neck and he was breathing very sharply. 'Hugh! Please wake up!'

He was scrubbing with his hands at something.

Scared now, she ran to Grandfather's door and knocked.

He was already up and awake, and had pulled on a large camel wrap-over dressing gown and grabbed hold of sturdy metal crutches from beside his bed. He seemed unaware of her embarrassed gaze as she took in the flapping empty pyjama leg.

'I didn't know whether to wake him – he's having a really bad dream,' she whispered.

The old man took in the fitful state of his grandson, then

he lowered himself down on the side of the child's bed.

'We don't want to shock him any more than he already is,' he told Sophie. 'You sit on the chair there in front of him, so when he opens his eyes he'll see you.'

He lifted the child's wrist.

'His pulse is very elevated, his breathing far too rapid,' he confided. 'Hugh!' he said in a loud voice. 'HUGH!' He repeated the name several times. 'Don't be afraid, Hugh, you're safe. Sophie and I are here with you, nothing bad can happen to you, I promise.'

Hugh stirred as if hearing something very far off. Sophie could just make out the words 'sea' and 'drowning' from his muttered words.

'It's all right, Hugh!' said the old man firmly. 'You are safe, Hugh!'

'Help me! Help me!' mumbled Hugh. He was trying to reach out, and he attempted to sit up.

Grandfather caught him gently in his arms. 'You're all right, Hugh! I'm with you.'

The boy seemed to stop fighting whatever invisible memory it was as his grandfather held him to his chest, rocking him. 'I have you, Hugh! You're safe!'

Hugh seemed to relax. 'Don't want to be torpedoed ... ship's going down,' mumbled the pale-faced boy.

'It's okay, Hugh lad!'

Sophie watched as Grandfather rocked his grandson gently. Her eyes were closing with sleep.

The old man held the boy for a long time until his breathing became easier and more relaxed. 'That's the boy, Neil, that's the boy!'

Sophie stirred. He had said her father's name – maybe Dad used to have nightmares and bad dreams too? She pretended not to have heard the slip of the tongue, and she helped Grandfather lower Hugh back into bed and she plumped up the pillows.

Hugh smiled sleepily at her. 'I had a really bad dream, Soph. I was a sailor on a ship and it was torpedoed and I was in the sea and trying to find some way out of the ship as it was sinking, it was ...' he yawned sleepily.

'It's over,' she assured him, and she pulled up the blankets. He was back in a sound sleep already.

She looked at Grandfather. He looked old and tired and worn.

'It's this war!' he said. 'It gives old men like me nightmares, it's no wonder it has got to poor Hugh.'

'He must have been thinking of Frank!'

'Yes, I suppose so!' he said wearily.

He was trying to stand up stiffly. The crutches had fallen half under the bed.

Sophie reached for them, then leaned forward to help him up. He put his hand on her shoulder for support.

'I've been a silly old fool,' he said slowly.

'I know you're doing your best for us,' mumbled Sophie.

'We could make it easier, Sophie!'

She understood what he meant.

'Do you think that the two of us could declare a truce and

call off the hostilities between us? Isn't one war enough?' he asked.

Sophie considered, then nodded slowly.

'I'm a stubborn old man, used to my own ways!' Grandfather said.

'I'm stubborn too,' she admitted. 'Dad often says so.'

'Now, I wonder where you got that from?' he whispered jokingly. 'Goodnight, Sophie,' he said, and he limped to the door.

She watched the tall figure stumbling off. 'Goodnight, Grandfather,' she said gently.

CHAPTER 26

The Londoner

Nancy came back at last. She looked thinner and older and she would not mention Frank and what had happened.

Sophie wondered what it was really like to lose a next-of-kin. How did you pretend to get back to normal? She searched the young housekeeper's washed-out face for a clue.

'Well, you managed then!' murmured Nancy.

'Grandfather cooked,' confided Sophie.

'Old bachelors can make good cooks – men can manage if they have to,' declared Nancy.

'Hugh wouldn't eat a thing!'

'Aye! Well, I'm here now, so we'll get things back on an even keel again.'

Nancy worked like a whirlwind around the house, cleaning and polishing furiously, as if she wanted to block out the events of the past eight days. The old man retreated to the peace and quiet of his study again, except for his twice-daily seafront stroll.

Summer was coming. Sophie could hear it in the cries of the seagulls that wheeled around the sunny blueness of the quay outside. The sea had lost its sharp salty tang and was becoming more gentle. Strangers were starting to promenade along the front, with excited dogs dragging them along this new-found territory. Grandfather had taken to wearing a blazer instead of his usual tweed jacket.

There had been three letters from Mum – well, not quite from Mum. One was from Nurse Harvey, describing how well Mum was doing and how she was moving to a different type of hospital, one that would teach her to do things again, help her brain to start working in a proper way and make her better. The second letter was very brief and just said that she had arrived safe and sound and was in the Montclare Ward. The other was from a woman called Rose who was a volunteer at the new hospital and was delighted to tell them all about her patient.

'Every week you will hear from me about your mother's progress,' she wrote. 'I know from vast experience the loneliness of separation from a loved-one and I will do my best to bridge that gap.'

Sophie wept, wishing that she was there with her mother, instead of a stranger called Rose.

'Are you two up to anything in particular?' enquired their grandfather after a late breakfast on Saturday.

'Nope!' they both replied.

'Then, come and follow me!' he said. 'I have to meet a man down at the harbour.'

The harbour was very quiet – all the boats had gone out fishing hours before. Grandfather waited impatiently until finally an elderly man came up to him. The two grey-haired heads bent close as if discussing some secret business.

The children leaned against the wall, soaking in the sunshine.

'Down to the beach!' ordered Grandfather suddenly. It was very stony and uneven and Sophie wondered if Grandfather would lose his balance.

But he stopped near the fishermen's cabins above the beach and pointed to a small rowing boat, one which Sophie hadn't noticed before. There were two seats in it and it was freshly varnished and amazingly clean – not a fish-head or rotten crab-leg to be seen.

The two of them looked it over. It was stained honey-brown and painted with a stripe of deep green.

'Well, what do you think of her?' shouted Grandfather.

It was then that Sophie noticed the small name plaque freshly fixed to the prow: *The Londoner.* At once she knew it was hers – theirs – it was meant for herself and Hugh.

A huge grin lit up Grandfather's face. Sophie had never seen him happy or smiling before. She felt a weight lift from her shoulders. This was his peace-offering.

'It's ours, Hugh!' she yelled.

Her young brother looked totally dumbfounded. 'Our own boat?'

She ran her hand along the smooth wooden side, caressing it. 'Ours!'

Sophie and Hugh reached their grandfather at the same time.

'Take care! Don't knock an old man off his feet,' he warned as they hugged him. His eyes searched Sophie's face for approval. 'Well, you like her then?'

Sophie could only nod. Tears welled up in her eyes. It was

the nicest thing anyone had ever given her in her whole life. 'Thank you, Grandfather.'

'You can't live in a place like Greystones and not have a boat,' he said. 'I think you'll be here for a while yet,' he continued.

Grandfather seemed to think the war was going to last. Sophie decided she would not let that knowledge disturb the pleasure of owning a boat.

Grandfather's friend, Mr Furlong, was searching around in his cramped little fisherman's storage hut. 'Here you go,' he shouted, and handed each of them an oar and a shiny silver oar-lock. Then he wandered back inside and came out with a rusty old paint can. 'You'll need this for baling her out. All timber will let water in, so mind you keep an eye on it!'

Hugh's ears were bright pink with excitement at the idea of having a boat of their own.

'Come on! Let's get her on the water,' said Sophie.

Grandfather gave an abrupt cough. 'Well, young lady! Do you think there is something we have forgotten?' he asked.

She racked her brain. The little boat looked perfect. Then in a flash came the image of Mr Kinsella up to his chest in water. 'Life-jackets! Oh, Grandfather, we must have life-jackets.'

Hugh was about to protest, not wanting any delays.

'I'm glad you remembered. Mr Furlong got two for me,' he stated firmly. 'They are under the seats. They must be worn at all times. Swimming lessons or not. Are we agreed?'

'Yes,' said the two of them solemnly. 'We promise.'

'That is an absolute unbreakable rule,' he said once more.

They nodded again, and Sophie reached in and pulled out the jackets. They put them on and zipped up.

'Ready!' called Hugh, and off they went.

Grandfather leaned against the wall watching them as they pulled *The Londoner* down to meet the tide. The water tried to push the small craft back on to the pebbly shore. It wasn't easy to launch her.

Mr Furlong came to their aid. 'You two hop in! I'll give you a shove.'

The seat was just about wide enough for them to sit side-by-side and fix an oar in each oarlock.

'Now, feel your balance. Just try to put the oar nicely in the water. That's right, young fellow. That's the way.'

Sophie's oar kept skimming the top of the water and she nearly fell off the wooden seat.

'Try to relax. Dip it in a wee bit more,' Mr Furlong advised.

It looked so easy but it was about half-an-hour before they managed to row together, both finally pulling in harmony. Twice they found themselves right back up on the beach again and needed another push. But they finally got the boat right out, away from the gritty sand on the shore-line.

They rowed out to where the water was out of their depth. It was cold and clear. Sophie could see under the water, rocks and stones that now had assumed strange, marvellous colours. She dabbled her hand in the water trying to catch the sunlight that danced beneath her fingers.

'Look, Soph. There's a sand-dab, and a crab!' Hugh was

leaning overboard, peering into the water.

'Take care, Hugh! You'll capsize us!'

The rest of the morning they rowed back and forth across the harbour. They were too nervous to go near the pier in case they bumped into it or into the boats moored near it, so they paddled along by the side of the slip. They each took turns rowing on their own – one giving orders and being captain and the other pulling *The Londoner* through the water. Grandfather was watching them still, smoking his pipe. He waved to them in the distance. 'Stay in the harbour!' he shouted. 'Be home for lunch!'

By lunchtime they both had blisters on their hands. Hugh had a huge watery blob on his palm.

'Don't burst it,' warned Sophie. 'It'll only make it sorer.'

'I don't care, Soph, I just can't wait to get back in the boat again. C'mon, let's get home for lunch – quick!'

They managed to edge *The Londoner* on to the North Beach and Mr Furlong helped them to pull it up the beach to where it was dry. They'd be back later, ready to row again. Just imagine – their own boat would be there, waiting for them.

CHAPTER 27

The Burnaby

On Sunday, Grandfather and Sophie and Hugh had been invited to tea by Aunt Dolly.

Grandfather had rooted out an old navy-and-grey striped blazer from his wardrobe. There was a slight smell of mothballs from it, but he didn't seem to notice. Hugh wore his new clothes and Sophie put on the floral-print skirt, to please the aunts, and her new white shirt.

They walked beside Grandfather up through the town, turning at last into the area called the Burnaby. Here, a winding cluster of leafy paths and roadways led to tall gabled houses that peeped out from behind climbing clematises and ivies.

Grandfather came to a halt outside an enormous white house, with green-painted gables and a matching green wooden veranda which skirted the lower half of the house. The house was called 'Four Corners'. Grandfather fiddled impatiently with the rusty catch on the gate.

'Dolly! We're here!' he shouted.

Sophie and Hugh could not believe it – imagine anyone in their family living in such a big house!

Their grandaunt appeared, flustered as usual. 'Welcome, children! Do come inside!' she said.

She led them through a dim cluttered hallway where the

sunlight spattered through the stained-glass of the door, to a large drawing room that overlooked the garden.

'Be careful not to knock anything over!' Sophie whispered to Hugh, giving him a nudge in the ribs, as her eyes took in the haphazard arrangement of comfortable floral-covered couches and the side-tables jammed with ornaments and pieces of silver and sparkling decorated cut-glass, which were probably worth a fortune.

Hugh's attention was riveted on the strange bent-up shape of a balding man, who was leaning sideways in a wheelchair. The room seemed to be centred around him.

'Darling George! Do wake up! Look who's here! It's Jerome and his grandchildren,' said Aunt Dolly brightly. 'They are called Sophie and Hugh – you remember, I told you about them. They were stuck in London during those awful bombings!'

The figure jerked, as if trying to upright itself, then from his twisted face, their granduncle smiled at them.

Grandfather walked forwards and clasped the gnarled-up hands firmly. 'It's me, Jerome! How are you, George?'

He beckoned to the children to come closer, sensing their discomfort. 'Your Uncle George had a stroke a few years ago,' he explained matter-of-factly. 'Come on, now! Come and say hello to him!' he ordered.

Hugh hung back behind Sophie.

'Pleased to meet you!' murmured Sophie nervously.

'Ne ... Neil's daughter,' Uncle George struggled to speak to her.

'Yes. That's right,' smiled Sophie.

'Always ... always liked Neil.'

'He's away someplace in Africa, fighting in the war,' said Sophie.

'Dolly and I went to Africa ... long, long time ago ...' He yawned, tired from the effort.

Sophie hoped that he would mention more about her father, but he didn't, his mind seemed to have wandered off to something else.

Hugh shook his hand quickly, then scampered off to the far side of the room.

A heavy awkward silence fell between them all as they sat formally in the drawing room. No one knew what to say and Sophie longed to escape. It was like divine inspiration when Aunt Dolly suggested she'd show them the garden and the grass tennis court while Maud organised the tea.

Aunt Dolly opened the french doors, and led them down some steps and through a maze of flower beds and rose bushes to a square of lawn, which formed a rather scraggly-looking tennis court. But the grass was freshly mown, and the smell tickled Sophie's nose.

'Maud touched up the marking lines and managed to find a net,' said their aunt, pointing to the narrow strip of painted grass and the thin droopy net blowing gently in the breeze. 'We thought, perhaps, yourself and Hugh might enjoy playing sometimes – if you were bored,' she added kindly.

'Thank you. Thank you so much. That would be very nice!' replied Sophie. There was no point in telling her that neither of them had a clue how to play tennis – it was not the sort of game children in Bury Street and Grove Avenue played. Still, she imagined it would be great fun trying to hit the balls over the net to each other.

'We used to have tennis parties here in the old days,' said Aunt Dolly, dreamily. 'It was lovely then. Susan and Teddy and their friends. It's such a shame to see it going to waste.'

'Did my father ever play tennis here?' asked Sophie, curious.

'What a question, my dear! Of course he did. I'll have you know, your father was a very good player. He could run rings round his cousin Teddy.'

Hugh interrupted them by making a sudden charge at the net, and swinging against it.

'Stop it, Hugh!' shouted Sophie, 'you'll break it!'

'Hugh, come inside with me, and we'll find you a racquet and some tennis balls!' offered their aunt.

Trust Hugh! Just when she was trying to get some information from her grandaunt, he had to come along and spoil it. Aunt Maud announced that tea was ready, so now they had to go back into that stuffy drawing room.

A large silver tray sat on a sturdy mahogany table. There was a plate of scones, and another plate with little triangular sandwiches – cucumber, shrimp paste and tomato. There was also a large fruit cake, and, best of all, fresh eclairs, bursting with cream.

Hugh licked his lips. 'Golly!' The children hadn't seen a spread like this since the war started.

'Well done, Maud!' cheered Aunt Dolly, and they all whole-heartedly agreed.

Aunt Maud took a plate and put three sandwiches on it, and filled a cup with tea, adding milk and sugar, then she went over and sat beside Uncle George. Sophie watched as her aunt broke the sandwiches into tiny pieces, which she fed to their uncle, carefully, bit by bit. Then she would raise the cup to his lips, encouraging him to swallow the tea. Once or twice it sounded like uncle George was nearly choking, which gave the children a terrible fright.

'Ever since his stroke, his swallow hasn't been the best,' explained Aunt Dolly. 'I don't know what we'd do without Maud.'

Grandfather interrupted his eating. 'Luckily for us all, Maud trained as a nurse and was able to come and help out.'

Aunt Maud was blushing now, a stain of red running from her neck right up the wide taut cheekbones. She suddenly appeared softer and less crow-like.

'It was the very least I could do,' she said, planting a light kiss on the patient's head. 'I was always very fond of poor George.'

Hugh had moved to sit close by Grandfather. He was rather nervous of the others.

'Terrible about Belfast!' murmured Aunt Dolly. 'They're trying to destroy the shipyards.'

'That's what they're hoping to do. Stop production. Stop the British Navy getting any more ships,' interjected Aunt Maud angrily.

Sophie ate as the adults began a long discussion of what Belfast was like before the war, in the 'good old days'. Hugh started to kick the corner of the couch, despite all Sophie's warning glances.

'Come on, young man! Let's get a breath of fresh air!' Grandfather stood up stiffly.

'Oh, I must fetch the racquets for the boy!' said Aunt Dolly, replacing her cup on the tray. 'Maybe the two of you will play?'

Uncle George had closed his eyes and seemed to be dozing. A tiny dribble of saliva ran down his chin. Aunt Maud dabbed it gently with a napkin.

'Dolly! You keep an eye on George, while Jerome and I have a bit of a walk. I'll get the racquets. I won't be long. Sophie, you might give Dolly a hand with the clearing up?'

Aunt Dolly and Sophie watched as the tall angular figure of the old man limped along beside the small lively boy, and the broad sturdy figure of Aunt Maud in her grey knitted suit. She carried two battered-looking tennis racquets under her arm, and was engrossed in conversation.

Aunt Dolly turned back from the window. 'They're discussing medical matters. She's telling him that George is getting worse.'

'I'm so sorry!' whispered Sophie.

'Jerome is a fine doctor,' said her aunt, 'he'll know what to do. You know, having the two of you to take care of – well, it's changing him. He'd shut himself off, away from people.'

Sophie did not like to disillusion her aunt by telling her

that her beloved brother still spent most of his day shut away in his study. Behind them Uncle George snored noisily, his head flopped forward.

'Come on! Let's put these tea-things away in the kitchen!' chided her aunt.

As they returned from the kitchen, Sophie noticed another, much smaller, room.

'That's the morning room. My piano is in it,' said Aunt Dolly, ushering her into the peace of the yellow-painted room. A small circular table stood in front of the window, and against the wall was a piano, an array of family photographs and portraits on top of it.

'Do you still play?' enquired Sophie, staring at the collection of black-and-white prints in front of her.

'Yes!' she nodded. 'I find it very relaxing. It makes me forget about all the bad things around me.'

'Me too! I mean, that's what happens when I sing.'

Her grandaunt's face creased into a smile, her blue eyes twinkling as she rummaged in the cluttered music box beneath the piano stool. 'Let me find some music! Now, let me see ...'

Sophie used the chance to study the photographs. They were mostly of a much younger dapper-looking Uncle George, and always beside him a shy gentle woman, her hair slightly frizzed as she squinted into the camera – it was Aunt Dolly. In two or three photos, a good-looking dark-haired young man and a slightly bored-looking girl posed in a family group with them.

'That's our Teddy and my beautiful daughter Susan,' her aunt informed her. 'She's married out in Canada and Teddy lives in Dublin.'

Up in the top corner, there was an old brown photograph of a vaguely familiar tall man. He was rowing a small boat, and beside him were two smiling girls.

'That's Jerome and myself and Maud. It was taken at Oxford. He took us out rowing on the river.' Both eyes travelled automatically to the next picture. 'That's Jerome's wedding.'

Grandfather was wearing a dark suit that looked too small for him and beside him stood a beautiful dark-haired girl in a long-sleeved beaded dress, a long veil flowing down over her bobbed hair.

'That's your grandmother, Julianne. She was English.'

'She's very pretty,' murmured Sophie.

'Yes, she certainly was. Jerome fell head-over-heels in love with her. He had just finished his studies when they met.'

'Tell me about her ... about them, please!' cajoled Sophie.

Aunt Dolly ruffled the music sheets, opened the lid of the piano and sat on the stool. 'He loved her very much – nearly too much, I'd say. Your Aunt Maud introduced them. It was love at first sight. They got married within a few months. Jerome was working in a hospital in London. He was a surgeon – they say he was very good. Then came the war!'

'The Great War?'

'Yes! Men were dying in their thousands. Dreadful wounds, dreadful injuries. Doctors and nurses were needed urgently.

I remember the stories Maud used to tell me – I fainted once, just hearing about it. Anyway, Jerome went off. But they had no proper operating tables, no equipment, no medicines – it was beyond belief what one human being was doing to another, or so we thought then. Maud drove an ambulance. Poor Jerome had to operate under appalling conditions.'

'Did he get shot or bombed?' interrupted Sophie. 'Was that how he lost his leg?'

'No!' said her aunt softly. 'Nothing glorious like that. He got gangrene!'

'Ugh!' Sophie recoiled. She had heard stories from her teacher in school. Mrs Kellett had told them of men crowded together, lying in pools of urine and blood, bitten by fleas, delirious, choked by mustard gas, and of rats the size of cats ...

'Another surgeon had to amputate his leg,' said her aunt with pain in her voice.

'What about Julianne?'

'They came back to live in Ireland, here in Greystones. Jerome had to give up his dream of surgery. He became a family doctor instead.'

Further along the wall, Sophie noticed another photograph of Grandfather and her grandmother and two small boys in funny sailor suits.

'Is that my dad?' enquired Sophie, peering at the picture.

'Yes,' nodded her grandaunt.

But then, who was the other boy, with the curly fair hair and cheeky grin? As if reading her mind, Aunt Dolly touched

156

the picture, 'And that is his brother Peter.'

Without thinking, Sophie let the words slip out. 'I didn't know Dad had a brother!' she gasped.

Aunt Dolly seemed to suck in a slow exasperated breath. 'Neil should have told you!'

'Where's Peter now? Does Grandfather still see him?' Sophie was breathless with excitement.

'Peter died, Sophie,' Aunt Dolly said, her eyes filling with tears, 'he drowned a few days before his eighth birthday.'

'Drowned!' exclaimed Sophie. 'On the beach?'

'No!' said Aunt Dolly. 'It was in the Cove. Neil and himself were down catching crabs. Those rocks are very slippery and when the tide turns the Cove becomes a trap. Well, nobody really knows what happened. Neil had gone farther along the rocks, and Peter was at one of those little rock-pools, and when Neil turned around and came back his brother was gone. His net and bucket were there still. Neil called and called, but eventually assumed his brother had just gone home on his own.

'But Peter wasn't at home. It was truly an awful, awful time. Jerome and Julianne were out of their minds with worry and grief ... then the searching and waiting until they found him.' Her aunt sighed heavily. 'It was so long ago, but sometimes it seems just like yesterday.'

'Poor Peter!' murmured Sophie. 'And my poor Dad.'

'It was so unfair, but your grandfather blamed Neil for what happened. Boys will be boys, George and I tried to tell him, but Jerome, I suppose, was too stubborn to listen. He didn't want to hear. Instead, he immersed himself in his work, became totally engrossed with medicine and his patients, and began to lecture to medical students. He had lost one son and seemed to want to block out and forget the other one.'

'And my grandmother?'

'Julianne adored Neil, but the loss of a child ... well, it's the wost tragedy that can befall a parent. She carried on, trying to make the best of things. But finally her health broke down and she died a few years later.'

'And so my Dad came to London.'

'There was nothing left for him here,' sighed Aunt Dolly.

'Then Dad met my Mum!' said Sophie.

'Jerome would not attend their wedding. Maud and George and I did our best to persuade him, but he just wouldn't go.'

'I know!' said Sophie.

'It was hard to understand why.'

Aunt Dolly suddenly looked old and tired and nervous. Fine lines ran in creases around her eyes, and Sophie realised that dark shadows gleamed through her pale skin.

'I've said too much. Always been my trouble – too much of a chatterbox, that's what George used to say.'

Sophie gave her elderly aunt a hug. 'Thank you for telling me about my family!'

Aunt Dolly smiled a watery kind of smile. 'Well, what about some music then?' She propped a sheet of music on the stand and began to play, her thin fingers skipping over the keys lightly.

Sophie recognised the tune at once. It was an old favourite

of her mother's and Dad had taught her the words.

She began to sing.

> *'After the ball is over,*
> *Just at the break of dawn,*
> *After the band is ended*
> *And all the stars are gone ...'*

Aunt Dolly nodded in approval as Sophie's clear voice filled the small room and drifted out through the open window across the garden. Sophie sang, thinking of her Mum and Dad and wishing that they were all together again. Why couldn't things be simple? Why did families have to be so complicated?

Outside, an old man stood listening, surrounded by rose-bushes.

CHAPTER 28

Forgiveness

For the next few days Sophie had so much to think about after the visit to Four Corners. It was as if her grandaunt had given her a very large piece of a jigsaw puzzle that had been missing. She began to understand her grandfather's grumpiness and awkwardness. Now she knew why he had been so angry the day Hugh had almost drowned. It was like history repeating itself, past and present mixed together fighting for attention.

The next weekend Greystones was crowded with visitors as it was the Whit bank-holiday weekend. The morning train had brought lots of people taking advantage of the good weather. They promenaded up and down the seafront, giggling and chattering. Grandfather refused to take his daily walk and sat at the front window, glowering at them all. The harbour and beach were invaded by an army of strange children laden down with buckets and spades, determined to enjoy themselves.

Then, shocking news broke the holiday atmosphere: Dublin's North Strand had been bombed by a German bomber in the early hours of Saturday morning! Searchlights and an anti-aircraft barrage lit up the dark night sky over the city, but to no effect.

Grandfather's face was grave as he told the children about

the bombing. In little more than half an hour thirty people had been killed and rows of cottages had collapsed, injuring many more.

Sophie couldn't understand how it could have happened. Ireland was neutral, they weren't even in the war. What was going on?

'Does this mean we have to start carrying our gas masks again?' asked Hugh.

Sophie hoped not. The two smelly rubber masks had been abandoned to hang on a coat peg in the hall since they'd arrived in Greystones, and she didn't fancy carrying them around again.

'We'll see!' said Grandfather, leaving his paper and going down to the kitchen to make himself a cup of tea.

Sophie glanced at his newspaper, reading the headlines. Then she saw a report on the effect the bombing had had on Dublin zoo. The bison had stampeded, the monkeys were frightened and the huge elephant had toppled over with the noise and shock of the bombs! Sophie giggled. She remembered the elephant in London zoo, grey and enormous with wizened leathery skin and a slow shambling walk and swinging trunk. Just imagine a great big creature like that toppling over! She laughed helplessly, unable to stop.

Grandfather returned with his cup of tea, and he looked at her strangely.

'What on earth is so funny?' he asked.

'It's the elephant ... toppled right over ... all the noise and the anti-aircraft guns and the searchlights and the poor old elephant ...' She was hysterical now, laughing and crying at the same time.

'Sophie, calm down,' said the old man. 'What ...'

But she was unable to stop – it felt as if she was toppling too, just like the elephant. Suddenly she was aware of strong arms lifting her. Grandfather drew her onto his lap and she buried her head against his chest. The strange mixture of crying and laughing shuddered through her. Hugh was standing nearby, his eyes wide, and he was saying words that she just couldn't make out.

Grandfather held her close. She could feel his strength.

'I'm so ... so scared.' The words came out, surprising her as they burst from her lips.

'It's all right, Sophie! I'm here. Don't be afraid. I will take care of both of you.'

From a deep, deep hidden corner of her heart, all the fear and loneliness gushed out of her, and still Grandfather held her close, stroking her hair, so that in the end she relaxed against him.

Later, she had hiccups, and Nancy brought her a cup of very sugary tea. Grandfather laid her down on the couch, fixed the tartan rug over her, and told her she must rest until lunchtime.

'I'll be in my study if you need me,' he told her. It was the same thing he had said many times since they had arrived, only now Sophie felt he really meant it.

CHAPTER 29

Bomber!

A few days later, Sophie was still tired. She had slept a lot but it was as if all her energy had drained away. Delayed stress and trauma, that's what Grandfather said it was. He told her that she had experienced things children were not supposed to be subjected to. He shook his head, thinking of the children of Europe.

He set off for his pre-breakfast walk, and she had heard the front door bang as he left.

Soon Nancy would start getting the breakfast. Hugh was probably still asleep. Sophie decided to stretch herself and get up – she'd had quite enough of being in bed.

She dressed quickly and stood at the wash-hand basin, splashing cold water on to her face to wake herself up, and lathering up the lily-of-the-valley soap Aunt Maud had given her.

Then she heard it! Her stomach churned at the familiar sound, her own pale face stared out at her from the mirror as the throb filled the air. She could almost feel it running through her blood. The heavy droning of an aircraft engine reverberated across the sky.

Hugh ran in, still in his pyjamas. Their eyes met.

'It's a bomber!' screamed Hugh. 'Where will we shelter?'

Sophie pushed the shutters back, pulled open the curtains

and looked out the window.

The sea glimmered, catching the sun's early-morning rays. She could tell it would be another sunny day – the sky was clear and blue already and there was very little cloud except in the distance. Then she spotted it – the wing – the nose – as it pushed out of the clouds.

'It's a Heinkel!' shouted Hugh. 'And it's heading right for us!'

Sophie watched as the rest of the plane cleared the cloud. It was behaving strangely, erratically, none of that steady sweeping approach like every other bomber she'd seen. Smoke curled from one wing.

'He's on fire! It's one of his engines,' shouted Hugh, leaping up and down with excitement.

The plane seemed to swing down over the water. What was he doing that for? Sophie watched, stunned, as the plane jettisoned its cargo. Two bombs dropped into the deep blue water below. He knows he's going to crash, she thought, as the bomber lurched wildly, straight in front of their house. The pilot was trying to get it to lift.

'Run, Hugh! Get out of the house!'

They fled downstairs and out into the hallway, shouting to Nancy who was working in the back kitchen to follow them. They ran down the driveway and out across the seafront, roaring and screaming.

Grandfather stood near the Cove staring out to sea, shading his eyes from the sunlight with his hands. 'That boy's in trouble,' he said grimly. 'He's trying to put her down safely and not do any harm. He's only got a few minutes at most.'

The plane had swung around once again and Sophie could actually see flames spurt from one side of it, and a face looking at her through the cockpit.

'He's heading for the harbour!' shouted Sophie, her heart pounding.

'Nancy, go and phone for an ambulance and get some help!' ordered Grandfather. 'Hugh, you stay with Nancy! Sophie, you come with me!'

Sophie ran along the seafront. Some of the houses were empty, as people used them only for summer holidays; others still had their shutters closed, blocking out light and sound. The hotel was busy evacuating the guests, clad in night attire, out on to the croquet lawn.

The bomber had just managed to clear the pier wall and was now trying to swing out over the dock and slipway from the harbour to the relative space of the North Beach. With every second it got lower and lower.

'Tell them get a boat out!' shouted Grandfather, limping behind Sophie.

Sophie ran as fast as her legs would carry her. The two old ladies who owned the chemist's shop were leaning over the wall in their dressing-gowns, and a man who was half-shaved stood nearby.

Sophie looked down at the beach. The fishermen were gone – they usually left just before sun-up. The beach was totally empty.

The plane was making queer sputtering noises. Behind

window panes, Sophie could see faces of people unwilling to be involved.

She scrambled down the slipway, jumping off it onto the rocks which led to the beach.

There was a boat there, turned upside down, but it was big and heavy. She'd never lift it! Anyway, they had no oars for it.

The Londoner lay where they'd left it yesterday. Mr Furlong had gone home by the time they'd come in, and had locked his hut, so they'd stored the oar-locks under the seat. She ran up to see if the two oars were resting against the side of the hut where they'd left them. They were.

Grandfather was shouting at the half-shaven man to come down and give them a hand.

At that moment a huge bang filled the air, the sound ricocheting from one side of the harbour to the other. The bomber dropped, nose first, into the sea.

'Come on, man! Help us get this boat into the water!' yelled Grandfather, being careful not to slip.

'I will!' said the man. 'But you know, Professor, I can't swim!'

The minute they got the boat onto the water, Sophie and Grandfather clambered in. The man waded in as far as he could, giving them an almighty shove to set them off. They both rowed as hard as they could.

The plane heaved up and down in the water. It had managed to straighten somewhat, and the waves tossed and tumbled over it.

'Come on, girl! We've got to reach them quickly.' Grandfather was all charged-up.

Sometimes one or other of them missed a stroke and an oar skidded over the water. Grandfather swore under his breath.

They could see the plane more clearly now. Greasy, oily water floated around it and lapped against *The Londoner.*

'If we get to them quickly, they might have some chance,' Grandfather stated. Then he passed her his oar.

'What are you doing?' she gasped.

He had taken off his shoes, and started to roll up his trouser leg. 'Taking off this darned thing!'

With a start, she realised what he was going to do. 'No, Grandfather! Don't!' she begged. 'It's too dangerous. You could be washed against the plane.' Already she could see sharp pieces of wreckage bobbing in the water.

'Please!' she remonstrated, trying to grab him and almost losing an oar in the process.

He was unstrapping his artificial limb. 'Keep the boat steady!' he shouted at her.

'Oh, don't go!' she cried.

'I've got to, Sophie. A fellow man needs help. They have parents and wives and children – we can't just let them die like this.'

Without another word, he dived, leaving his jacket, shoes and artificial leg abandoned on the floor of the small boat.

The Londoner rocked wildly for a second, but Sophie managed to steady her.

Grandfather had disappeared under the water. Sophie could see what looked like part of the cockpit. She tried to row closer. There was a hand pummelling against the heavy glass. Grandfather reappeared near her. Sophie had not realised what a strong, powerful swimmer he was.

'There's two or three of them!' he told her, before swimming off to the far side of the plane. He leant on the bomber, trying to roll it over a bit. As it began to turn ever so slightly, more of the nose became visible. He was trying to help the pilot to open the cover. Suddenly it gave and a blueish-looking face gasped for air, and clutched wildly at his rescuer, before starting to free himself and ease himself into the water.

'*Danke! Vielen dank!*' muttered the German pilot through chattering teeth.

'The next one is bad!' shouted Grandfather. 'Try and bring the boat closer, Sophie!'

The sea water was suddenly stained a pinkish red. He was so young-looking. He reminded her of a prince from a fairy story, with his blond hair and eyelashes. The old man was pulling him forward.

'Help me pull him out!' he ordered the pilot. 'We'll try and lay him across the boat.' Maybe the German didn't speak any English.

'*Ja! Ja!*' he agreed. He treaded water, keeping himself afloat as he helped drag his injured mate out of the plane. The injured man was moaning, saying words that Sophie couldn't understand, and a huge gash ran from his shoulder to his wrist. They both swam with him to *The Londoner.*

Sophie leant over to one side, praying that she wouldn't capsize, as she tried to get him into the boat. He kept rolling off, back into the water. She grabbed frantically at his belt. Eventually there was more of him in the boat than out. The bottom of the boat was filled with inches of water, and she wished that she had someone along to bale out for her.

Grandfather had swum back to the plane again.

This time he was saying a prayer.

> *'Our Father who art in heaven,*
> *Hallowed be thy name ...'*

The exhausted German, floating beside him, joined in:

> *'Vater unser, der Du bist im Himmel,*
> *Geheiligt werde Dein Name ...'*

The plane seemed to be tilting, filling with water. Both men swam away from it, and Sophie rowed backwards for a bit, trying to avoid being sucked under.

'Nothing more we could have done! A broken neck, I'd say. Anyway, he's gone!' said Grandfather resignedly.

They watched as the German plane disappeared beneath the waves.

CHAPTER 30

Safe Harbour

'Ahoy there! Professor!' Sophie looked up. A boat was coming towards them, the sound of its motor carrying across the water.

She had never been so glad to see anyone in her life. She'd been worried that she might not be able to row with the weight. The men in the motor boat hoisted the German airman and Grandfather easily on board, then they came right alongside her.

'You okay?' asked one of them. She nodded.

'Take this! That's the girl!' he called, tossing her a rope, which she pulled through the heavy circle of metal on the prow, coiling some of it around the seat.

'We'll tow you in!'

Relief washed over her – her arms and neck ached, and she felt shaky inside.

The young man moaned as they began to move. Sophie covered him with Grandfather's jacket.

'*Meine Mutter! Mein Vater!*'

It sounded to her like he was saying 'mother' and 'father'.

'Don't worry, we'll tell your mother and father,' said Sophie. 'You are in Ireland. You are safe!'

A large crowd had gathered on the beach, Hugh and Nancy among them. They all began to clap as Sophie and

Grandfather got out of the boats. Two or three boys started to giggle, staring at Grandfather's thigh like he was some kind of freak. Nancy managed to find a towel and she wrapped it around him.

Silence descended on the crowd when the young injured German was lifted onto a stretcher and carried up to the road to a waiting ambulance. His blood lay spattered all over *The Londoner*.

Some people jeered and booed when the German pilot stepped off the boat onto the beach. Grandfather glared angrily at them. Sophie felt such pity for the pilot – his face was ashen, and he looked cold and miserable. One of his friends was dead, the other badly injured and he was left to face the music on his own. A local Garda stepped forward and was reading him something. The German just nodded blankly.

'What will happen to him, Grandfather?' Sophie asked.

'They are arresting him,' he said, wearily.

'Will they shoot him?'

'Oh no! Nothing like that! He'll be sent to the internment camp in the Curragh. He'll be kept there for the rest of the war. Probably the best thing that could happen to him!'

'Oh!' said Sophie.

The German was back now, bowing to her, thanking her for rescuing him. He shook Grandfather's hand warmly. 'Oscar Furtinger,' he said. They supposed that was his name. 'Und Dieter!' he said, pointing to the ambulance.

The crowd watched as both Germans were taken away.

Grandfather refused to go to the hospital. 'All I need is some dry clothes, a hot drink and a glass of my best whiskey, and I'll be fit as a fiddle again.'

'No point in trying to convince him,' said Nancy. 'He's a stubborn, difficult man! He'll do what he wants in the end. Come on, Professor, we'll get you home.'

Water dripped from Grandfather's hair and beard and from his clothes. He had strapped his leg back on and picked up his walking stick. He was helped up, then he reached for Sophie. 'Let me lean on you, girl. Come on, home we go!'

The little party set off across the stones for Carrigraun, Nancy holding Hugh's hand.

'You're a brave lassie, Sophie,' said Grandfather quietly in her ear, admiration in his voice.

'I was proud of you too out there,' said Sophie.

'Out there I didn't feel old,' he told her. 'All I could think of was rescuing those poor boys – I kept thinking it might be Neil ... somewhere out there ... in all this madness.' He stopped, and looked at her. 'Do you think we've left it too late, Sophie?' he asked.

She understood immediately. She shook her head. 'It's never too late ...'

There was no telling how long the war would last or, for that matter, how long she and Hugh would be here, but at least now things would be different. Perhaps Grandfather was finally ready to make peace with his son and end those long years of family bitterness.

'We'll have to write to your mother's hospital,' Grandfather announced. 'Find out her exact condition. You know, Sophie, sea air is beneficial in most convalescent cases.'

Sophie's heart soared. She looked back over Greystones, with its beaches and cove and blue, blue sea, and she realised just how much she had come to love this place.

'Come on, Sophie,' said Grandfather gently. 'It's time we all got home to Carrigraun.'

OTHER BOOKS BY
MARITA CONLON-McKENNA

THE BLUE HORSE
Winner Bisto Book of the Year Award

When their caravan burns down, Katie's family must move to live in a house on a new estate. But for Katie, this means trouble. She must fit into a new life, but will she be accepted?

Paperback £4.50

NO GOODBYE
When their mother leaves, the four children and their father must learn to cope without her. It is a trial separation between their parents. Each of them misses her in their own way, but the big question for all of them is: Will she come back?

Paperback £4.50

ALSO FROM THE O'BRIEN PRESS

KATIE'S WAR
Aubrey Flegg

Katie's father returns shell-shocked from the First World War and she helps him recover. Now the Irish Civil War is breaking out and the family's loyalties are split – should Katie side with Father or adopt Mother's nationalist beliefs? Then Katie and the Welsh boy, Dafydd, find a hidden arms cache – can they make a difference after all?

Paperback £4.99

SISTERS ... NO WAY!

Siobhán Parkinson

Winner Bisto Book of the Year Award

Cindy does NOT want her Dad to remarry after her mother's death – especially not Ashling's Mum. No way do these two want to become sisters! Two diaries record the events, from two very different teenagers. A flipper book, this story deals with teenage life in an amusing and unusual way.

Paperback £4.50

MISSING SISTERS

Gregory Maguire

Alice lives in a New York orphanage in the fifties. She discovers that there is a mystery surrounding her background and she sets out to solve it – and to meet the mysterious girl called Miami.

Paperback £3.99

Send for our full colour catalogue